AF395045

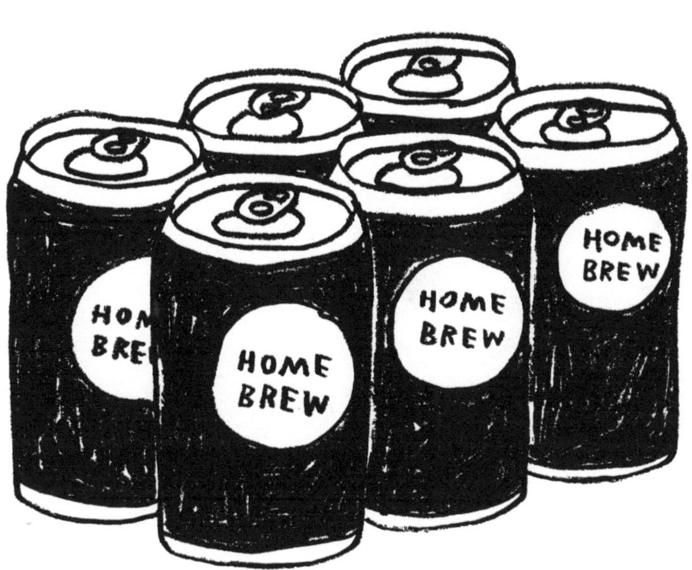

HOME BREW
HOME BREW
HOME BREW
HOME BREW

HOME BREW
ISSUES 1-6

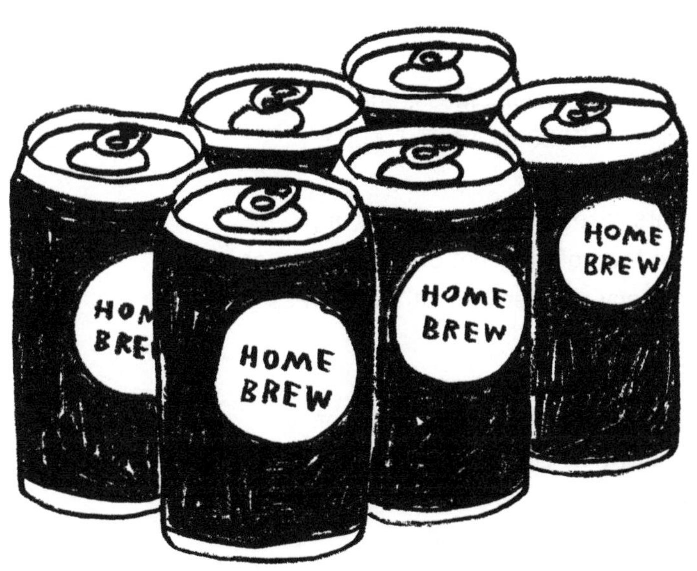

MOODS, MESS, AND MISTAKES

ADAM J. KURTZ

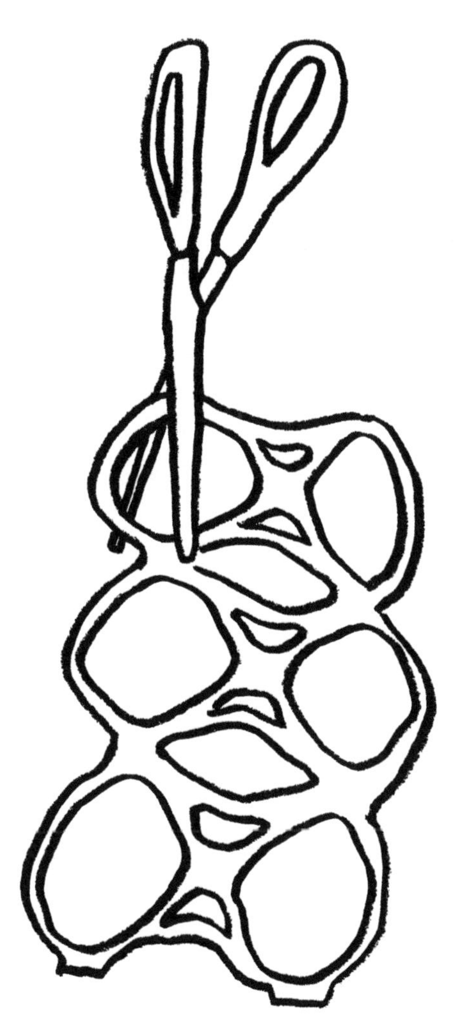

CONTENTS

FOREWORD

It's way more fun to receive a zine than a business card and a zine called TALKING ABOUT FEELINGS was sort of Adam's business card when I first met him in late 2011.

He was visiting Portland (where I live) and we knew of each other through the internet (Instagram?? Twitter? I have no idea...the internet felt a bit smaller even though that was only not even ten years ago). We had a nice time talking in our studio and before he left, he gave me a copy of his zine as a sort of thanks/goodbye gift. I LOVE using zines as thanks/goodbye gifts! It's such a sweet move.

A few months later, he mailed me HOME BREW #1. It was sort of a perfect little zine that really cemented my appreciation of Adam and all of the things that he does. HOME BREW contained many of my favorite things: scraps of found paper! Handwriting combined with photos! Disconnected thoughts that actually were connected! Jokes that were not supposed to be jokes! Funny things that actually were sort of serious! It quickly turned into a favorite zine to share whenever I would travel around giving zine workshops at different schools, and it became a favorite zine of my workshop

HOME BREW

students too. That zine was relatable and accessible and it made them want to make zines (BRILLIANT).

It also embodied what I was constantly preaching at these workshops: tell your story, don't over think, just make, share and make some more. REPEAT.

The original HOME BREW #1 was stolen along with the rest of my zine workshop supplies as I was getting ready to travel to an event in Chicago in 2012. My car was broken into and I am sure the thief was SUPREMELY disappointed when they realized that the suitcase they just scored was filled with paper and staples.

I posted about my sadness on the internet (because that is what you do) and shortly after, I received zines from people that I knew and people that I didn't know, which quickly replenished my zine collection. Adam sent me more of his zines, along with other zines from his own collection, to add to the generous pile.

That's just something else about zines... once you start making them, you become part of this generous community that will keep you supplied with zines. Zines can be whatever you want them to be which can either be very freeing or very scary (but don't let it be scary. What's really scary is if you don't make anything at all).

Zines are stellar paper container organizers to showcase your collections, obsessions, personal stories, illustrations, reviews, complaints, and/or accolades and Adam used this paper container to really work out ideas that were living in his head / sketchbook / post-its / texts and made them REAL, simply by organizing them into zines and sharing them.

Now go and make your OWN zines! Don't let your ideas stay in your head / sketchbook / post-its / text. Pour them onto some pages, photocopy and share.

Your voice is needed and welcomed.

GO MAKE STUFF OKAY?

–Kate Bingaman-Burt
Illustrator, educator, and super zine enthusiast

INTRODUCTION

I started making zines because I was desperate to create something real: a home for the art I was sharing on the internet and a tangible outlet for the "moods, mess, and mistakes" holding space in my brain.

The first issue partly documents a trip to Portland for a three-day interview at an experimental ad school that I hoped would change my life in a period of directionlessness (I didn't get in). By the second issue, I'd moved to New York, and by the third I was in my first serious relationship. These were my visual diary mixed up at home and released in small batches.

HOME BREW grew with me through my twenties, reflecting life as it happened in the ways I knew how to process. For me, that took the form of doodles, fake books, pill bottles, bits of conversation, plenty of internet, paper in all forms, and other recurring ideas that didn't always feel obvious at the time.

There are many reasons to not publish this collection. Much of it is awkward, bad, or embarrassing. Plenty of it represents moments in time and versions of myself that I no longer identify with. Besides, as the very first page makes clear: "Not everyone needs a memoir."

Despite the foreshadowing, nearly a decade later, I'm grateful for this paper trail. HOME BREW's recurring themes and ideas have ultimately found homes elsewhere in my work. These scraps and rough drafts document the creative growth of an artist trying to find their voice, and a person trying to find their place. Today, I am… getting closer.

From issue 2 onward, HOME BREW came packaged with an assortment of extras like stickers, pin badges, and balloons. These "sad loot bags" helped soften the blow, because even when things are hard, there's still so much joy to be found in the ephemera of being alive. At the right time, almost anything can be that good luck charm that helps us pull through.

I've always believed in the magic of making something from nothing. A book is six zines is twenty-four pages is a single image printed as a postcard. For me, that belief has led to a body of work that's not always good, but always rooted in who I am and the experiences of my life along the way. All I can hope for is to continue the work of processing my existence and communicating with others, with whatever I've got, in any medium I can, until I can't.

–Adam J. Kurtz

HOME BREW

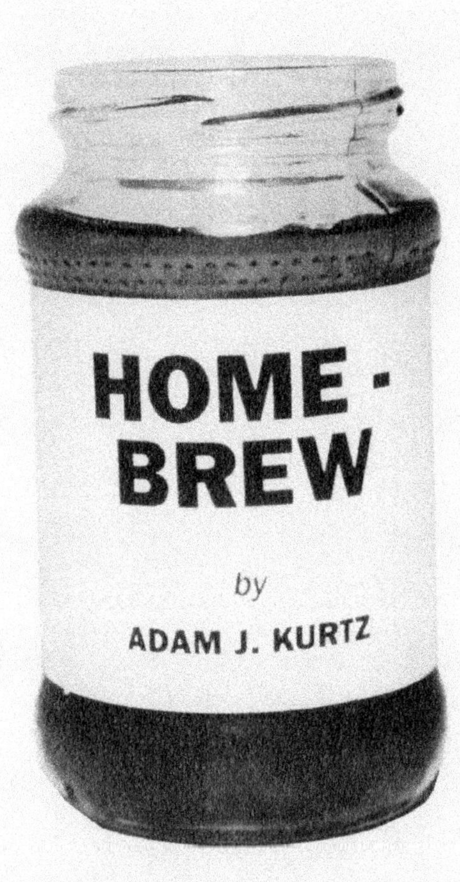

HOME -
BREW
by
ADAM J. KURTZ

HOME BREW

HOME - BREW

MOODS, MESS, & MISTAKES
REGARDING PEOPLE, PLACES, &
THINGS.

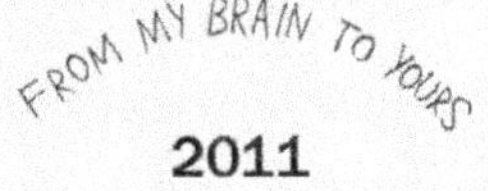

2011

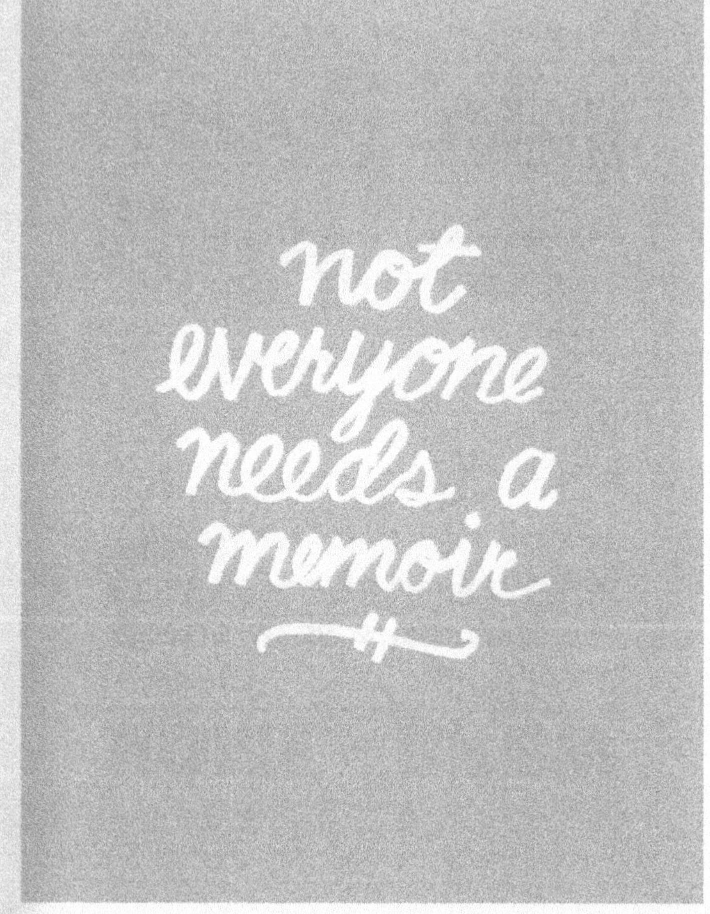

HOME BREW

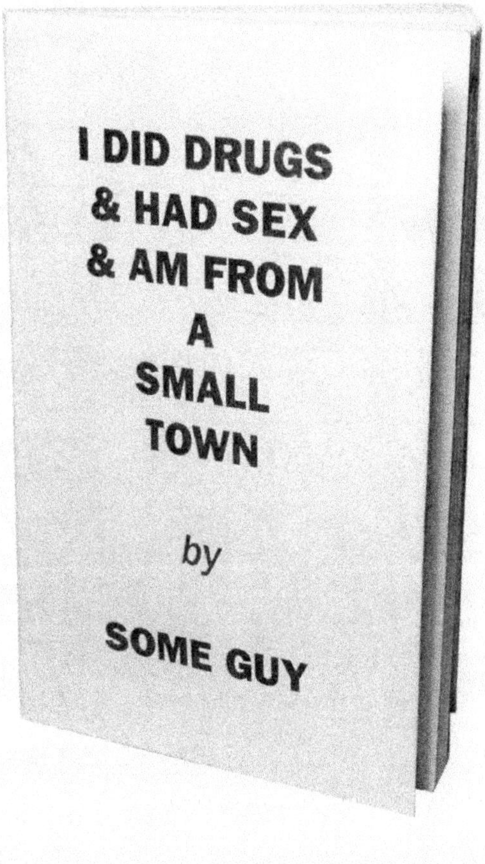

I DID DRUGS
& HAD SEX
& AM FROM
A
SMALL
TOWN

by

SOME GUY

"I'M IN A HORRIBLE MOOD
RIGHT NOW I WILL TELL
YOU ALL ABOUT THINGS
MAYBE OR MAYBE WHO
CARES ABOUT MY MOODS
OR THE PEOPLE OR THIS
SCHOOL OR PORTLAND
OR LIFE."

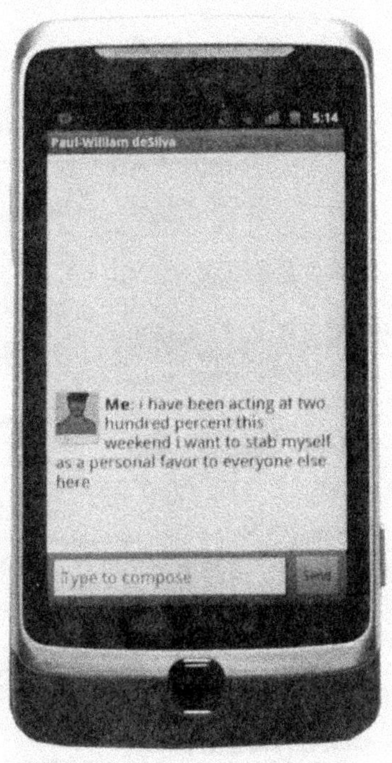

IF ANYONE NEEDS ME,

I WILL BE :(:(:(IN SELF-PITY

THAT THING WHERE A SHOW YOU REALLY LIKE ON HULU IS APPARENTLY NOT POPULAR ENOUGH FOR REAL COMMERCIALS SO IT'S ALL SPOTS FOR NON-PROFITS.

HOME BREW

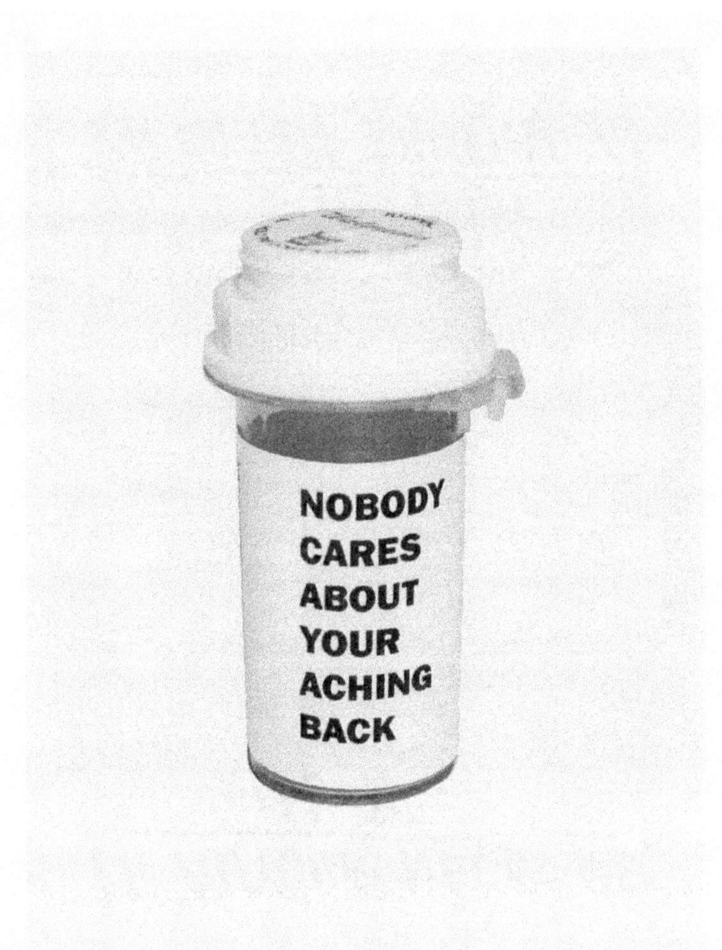

NOBODY
CARES
ABOUT
YOUR
ACHING
BACK

IF ANYONE NEEDS ME, I WILL BE:

I ALSO

"ACTED AND REACTED IN A MANOR"

BUT IT WAS DIFFERENT

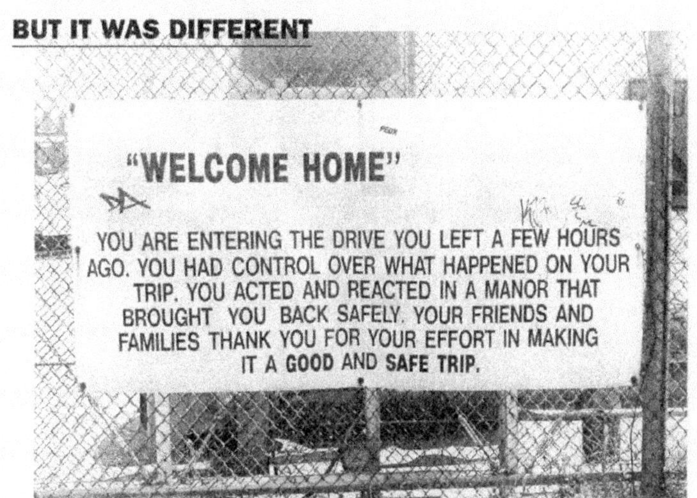

THAT'S
RIGHT
THAT'S
RIGHT
THAT'S
RIGHT

I KNOW THATS RIGHT

I KNOW THATS RIGHT

I KNOW THATS RIGHT

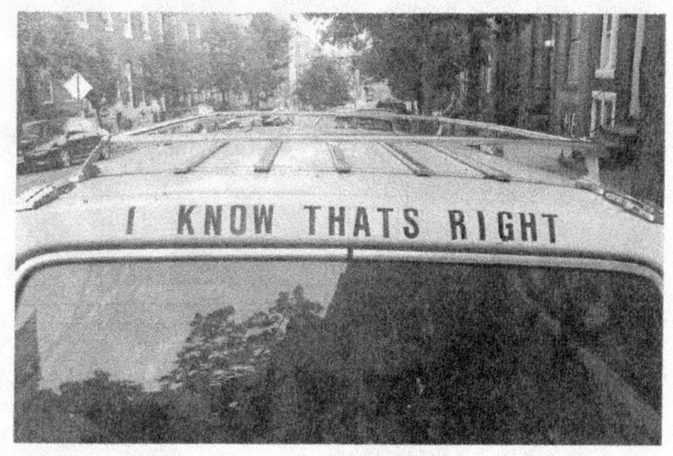

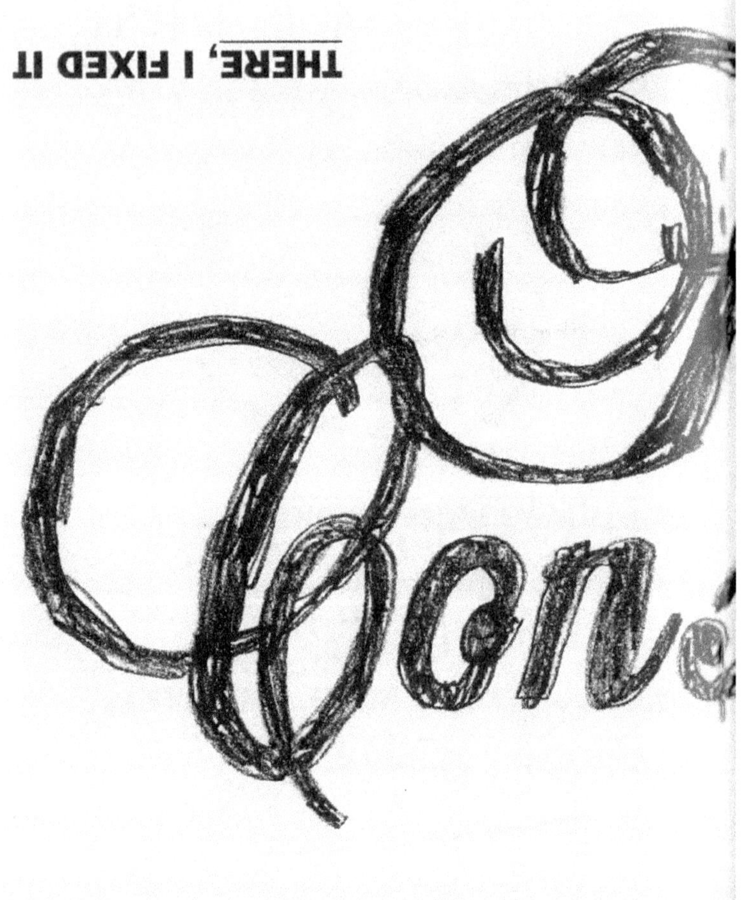

HOME BREW

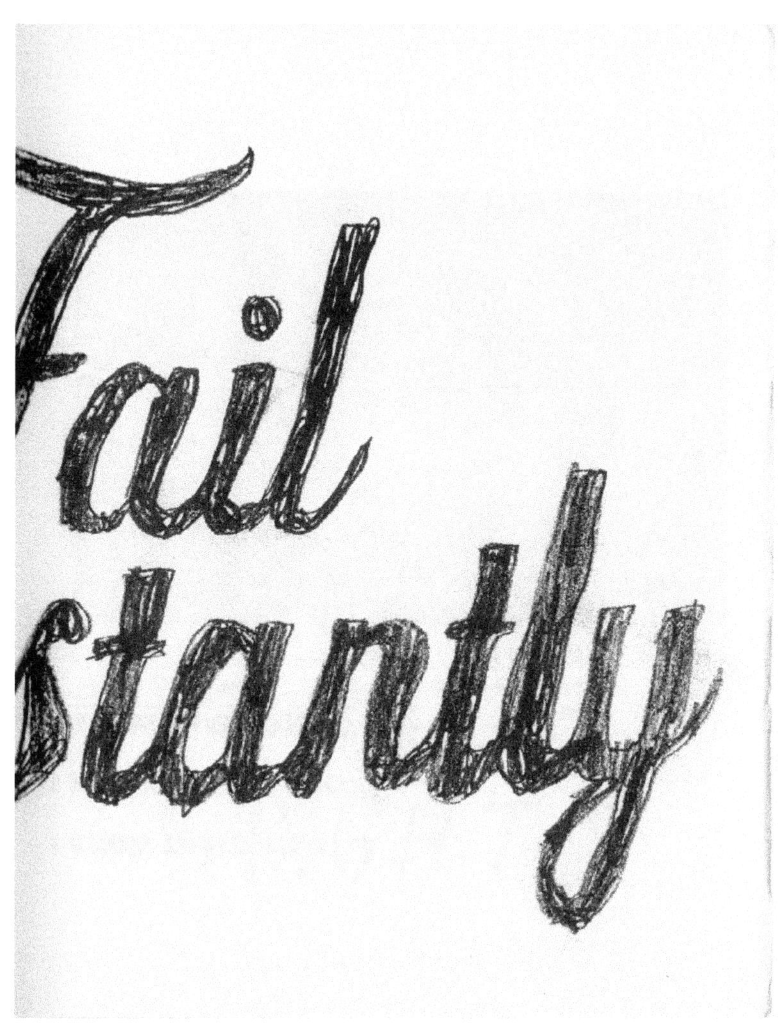

Fail
stantly

THE EXACT MOMENT
WHEN I REALIZED

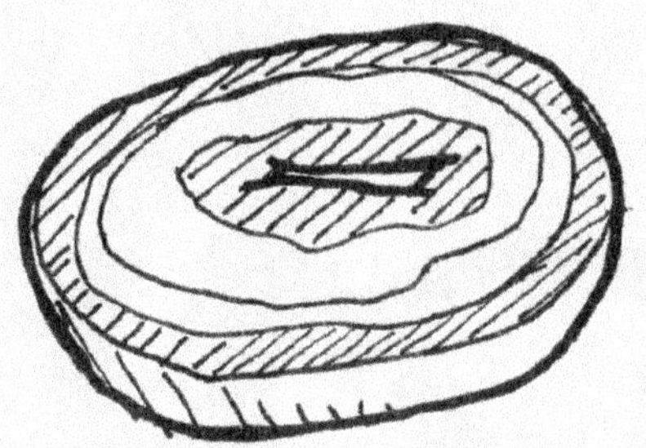

MY RAISIN BAGEL
WAS, IN FACT,
BLUEBERRY...

I LEARNED A LESSON
ABOUT "GETTING WHAT YOU WANT"

I ALMOST DIDN'T EAT IT
BUT IT WAS BANANA BREAD
SO I HAD NO CHOICE

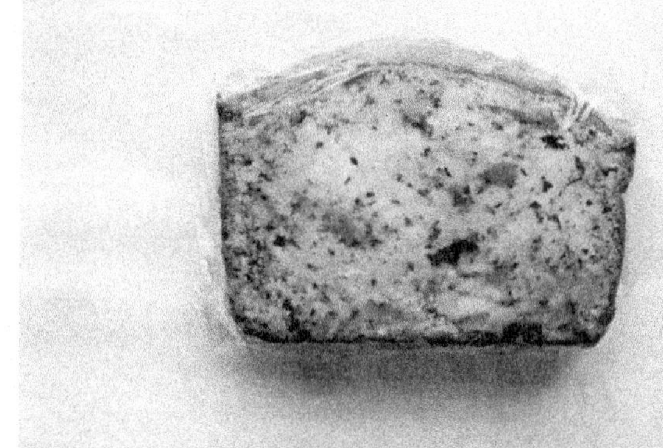

THIS IS WHERE
I WILL PUT ALL
MY GOOD IDEAS:

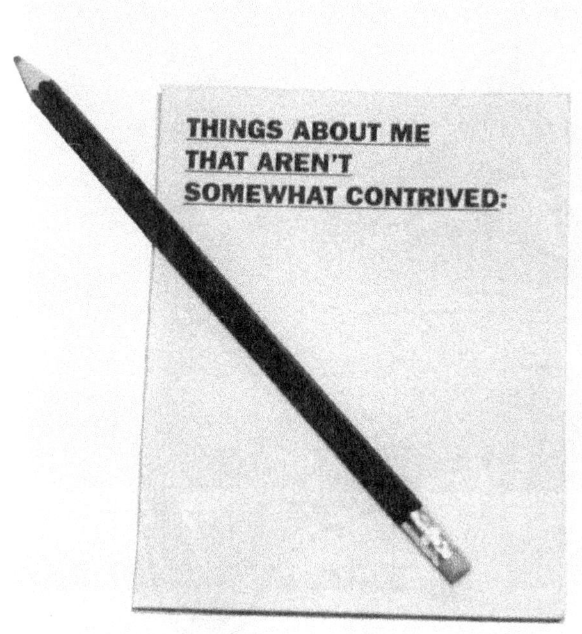
THINGS ABOUT ME
THAT AREN'T
SOMEWHAT CONTRIVED:

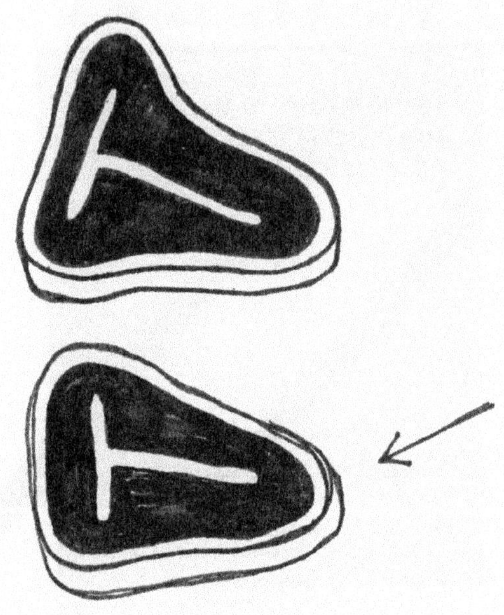

HOME BREW

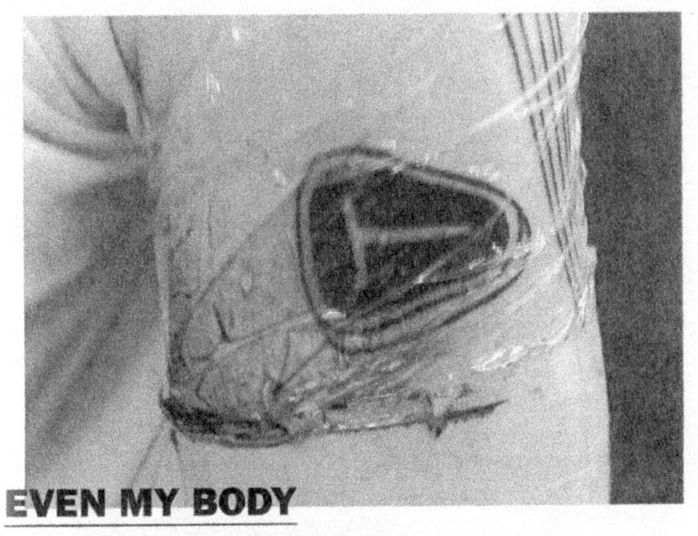

EVEN MY BODY

WAS IN ON THE JOKE

THE MAN AT THE
COUNTER ASKED IF I
"DID MODELLING"...

WHICH WAS
EXTREMELY FLATTERING.

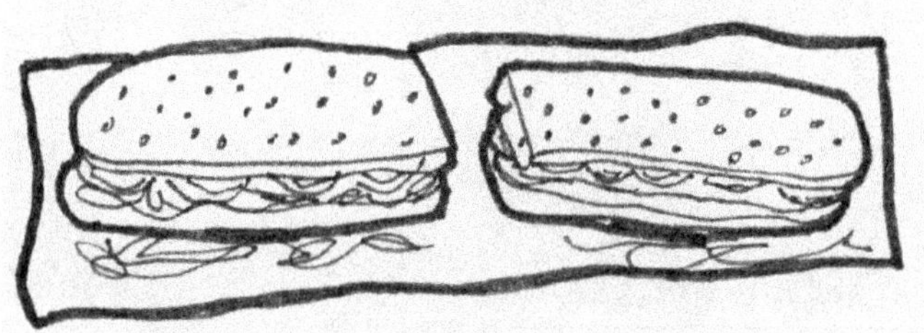

THEN I ATE MY
FOOTLONG SANDWICH...

WHICH WAS NOT.

I LOVE SANDWICHES

WHICH IS WHY

I HATE SUBWAY

Store #35703   LKU 09/22/11 12:13:33
Subway Sandwiches & Salads
7050 friendship rd

410-356-5479
Trans# 252 Clerk 300 chandra
Dwr1 TRDT 092211 Reg-ID MAIN
                 Receipt # 0000340218
--- ITEM --- QTY   PRICE MEMO PLU
TUNA   fr 1 T $ 6.49   10217

           SUBTOTAL $ 6.49
           Sales Tx $ 0.39

TAKE-OUT **TOTAL $ 6.88
CredCardAMT TEND $ 6.88

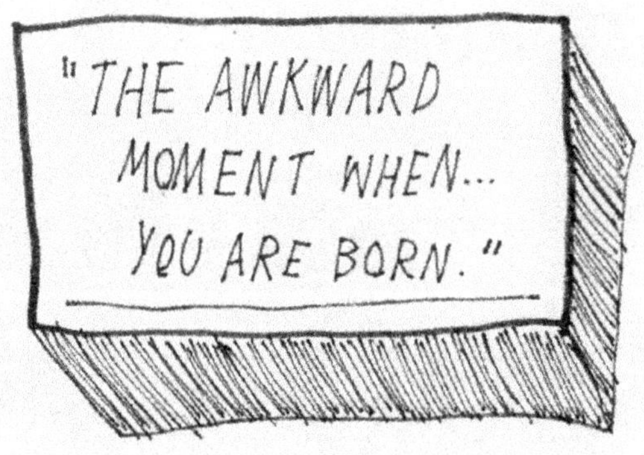

HOME BREW

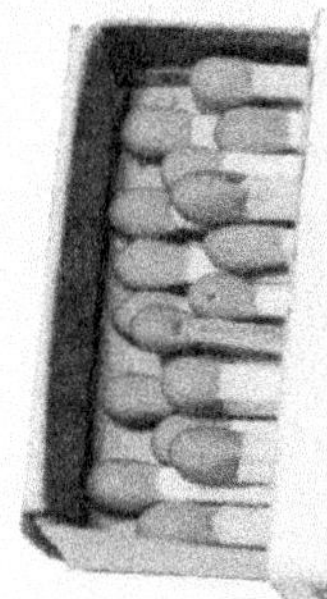
I WAS PLAYING WITH
MATCHES THIS WEEK,
WHICH WAS WEIRD...

WHERE WAS MY
LIGHTER FOR ALL OF
THIS?

HOME-BREW

MOODS, MESS, & MISTAKES
REGARDING PEOPLE, PLACES, &
THINGS.

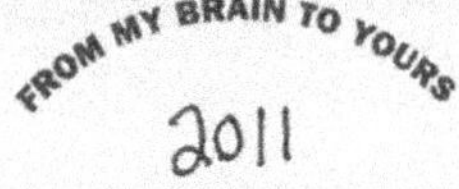

HOME BREW

HOME BREW

HOME BREW

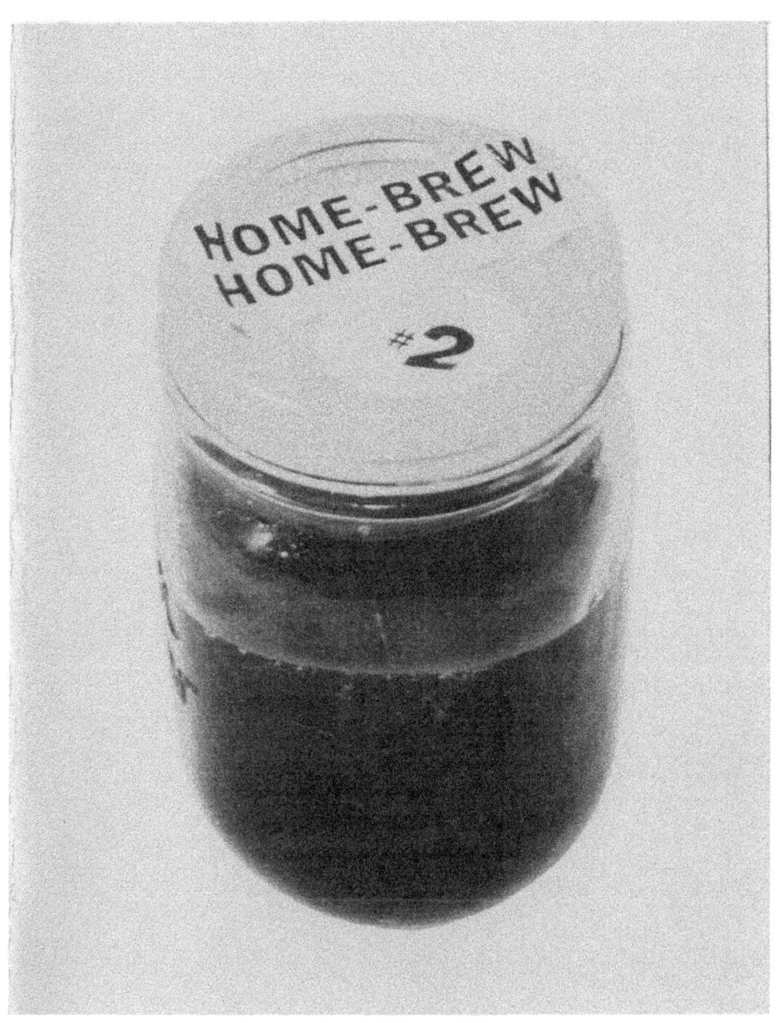

HOME-BREW
HOME-BREW
#2

HOME BREW

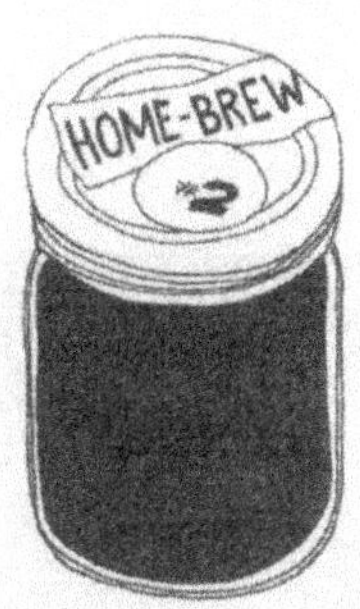

MORE MOODS, MESS & MISTAKES REGARDING PEOPLE, PLACES & THINGS
BY
ADAM J. KURTZ

FROM MY BRAIN TO YOURS
2012

I LOVE THAT YOU ARE ONLINE
I LOVE THAT I CAN SEE YOU
I LOVE WHAT YOU ARE WEARING
I LOVE WHAT YOU HAD FOR LUNCH
I LOVE YOUR NEW HAIRCUT
I LOVE BEING CONNECTED
I LOVE THAT YOU ARE ONLINE

RIGHT NOW

HOME BREW

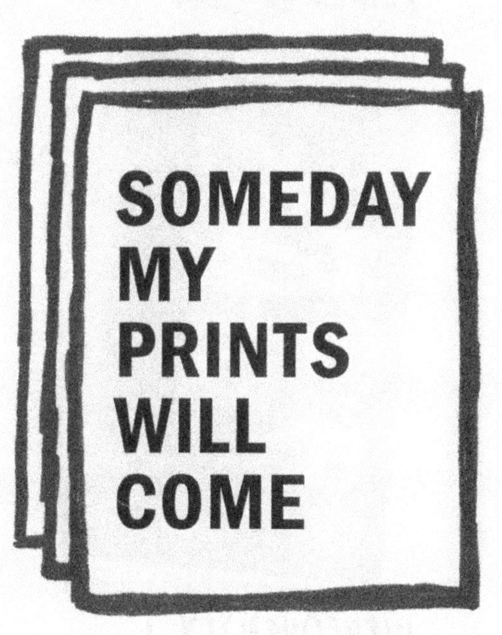

SOMEDAY
MY
PRINTS
WILL
COME

IT COST $110 TO
REMEMBER JUST HOW

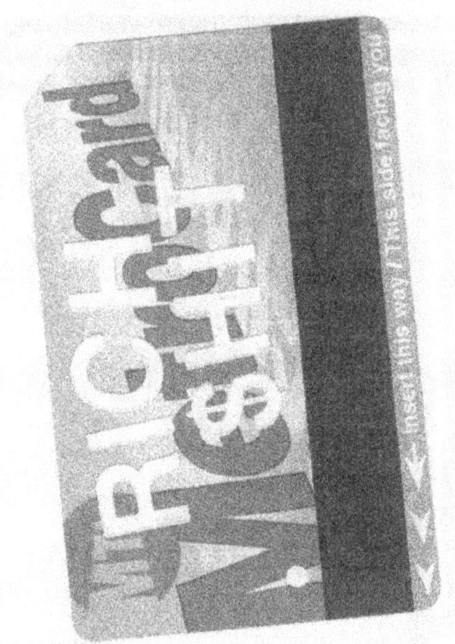

INFREQUENTLY I
LEAVE MY APARTMENT

HOME BREW

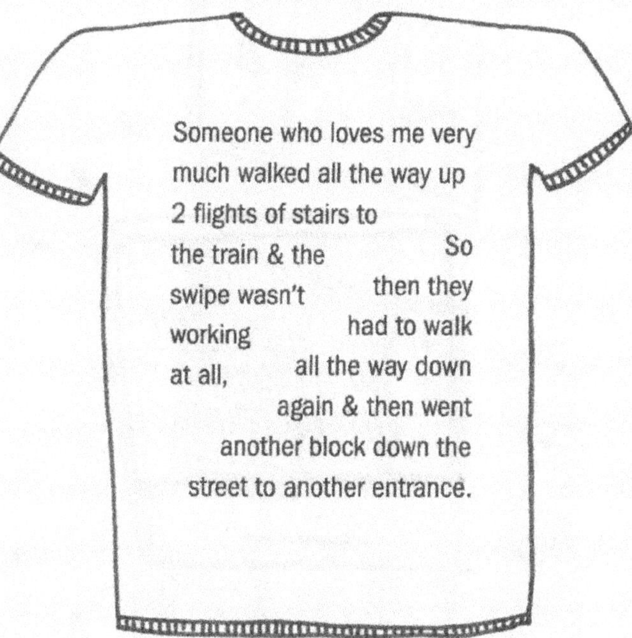

SOUVENIR
SUGGESTION

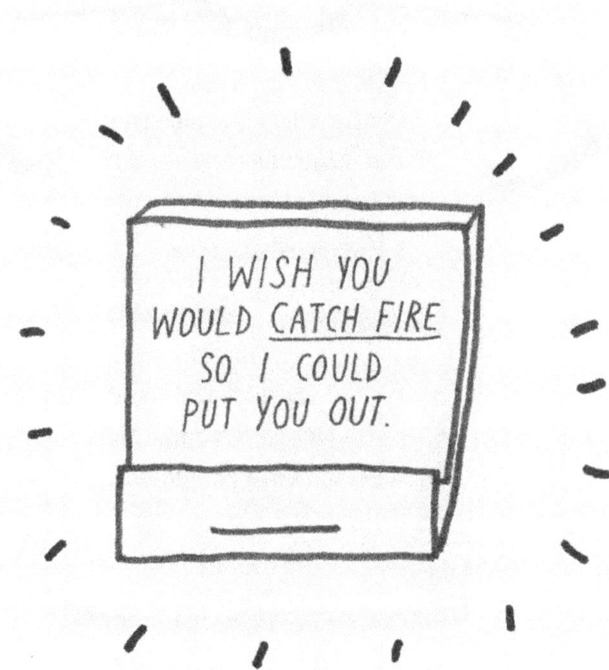

HOME BREW

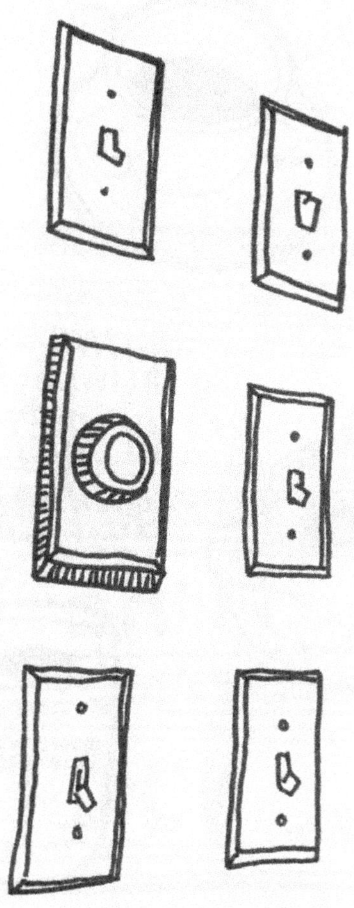

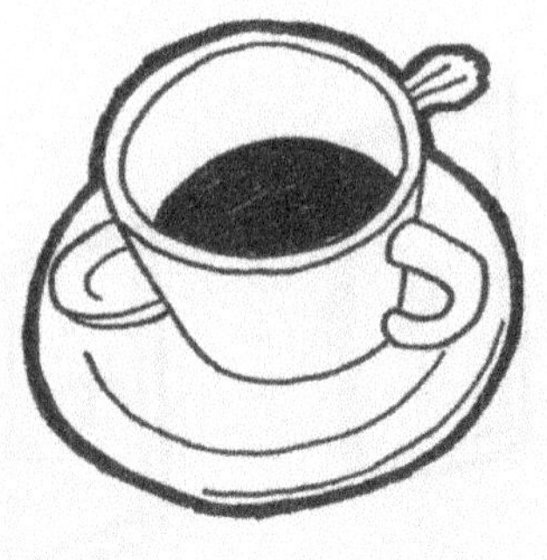

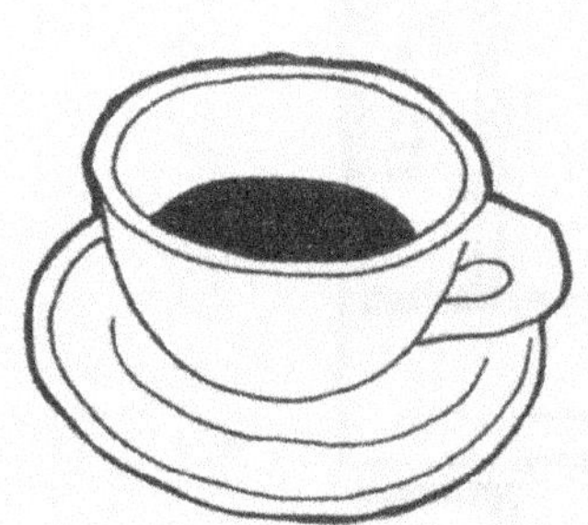

THREE CUPS
OF COFFEE IS
NOT ENOUGH

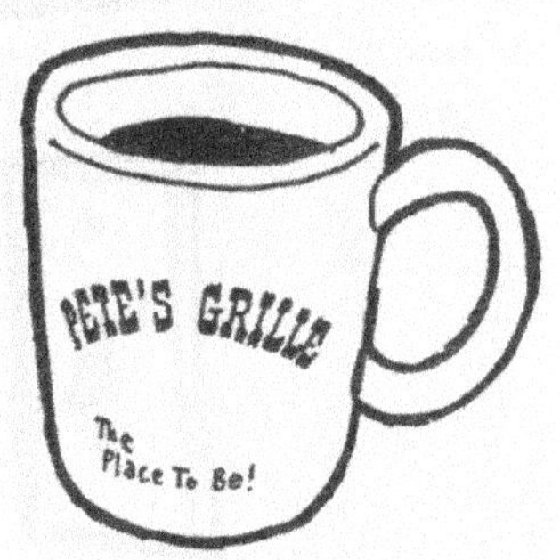

HOME BREW

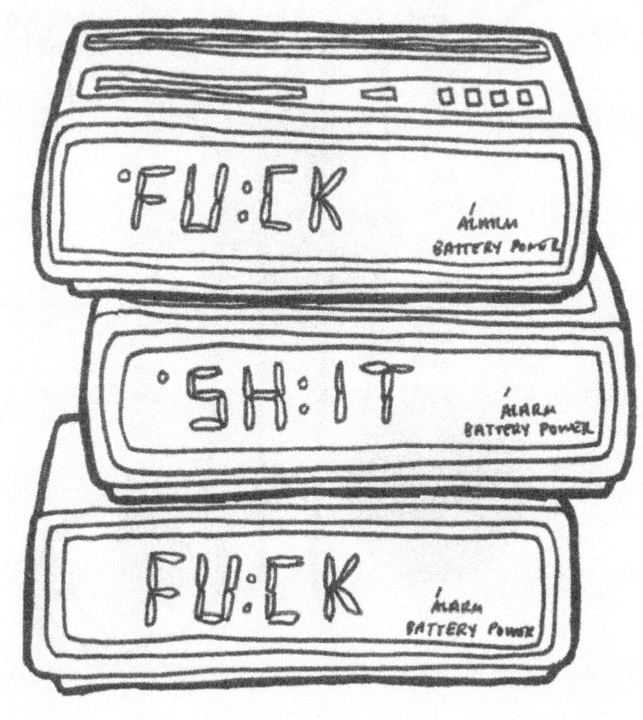

FU:CK
ALARM
BATTERY POWER
SH:IT
ALARM
BATTERY POWER
FU:CK
ALARM
BATTERY POWER

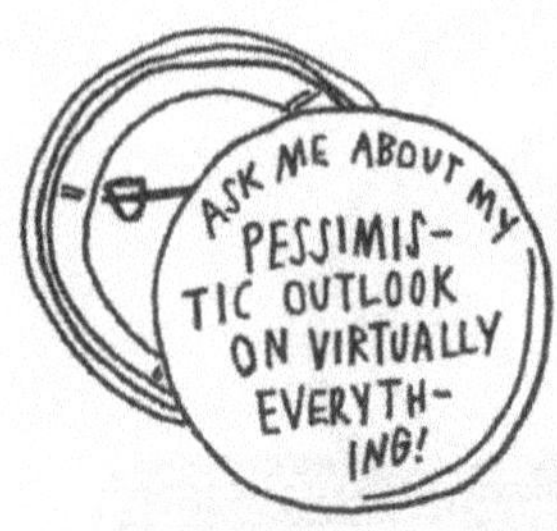

Please

ASK ME WHAT MY TATTOOS "MEAN"

I'D MUCH RATHER BE SLEEPING!

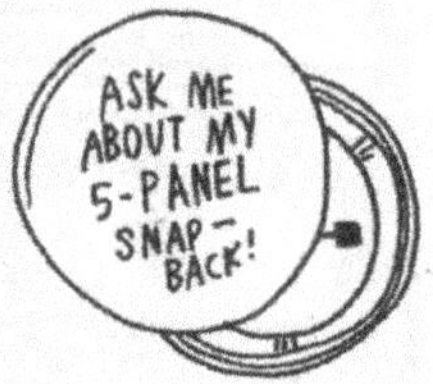

HOME BREW

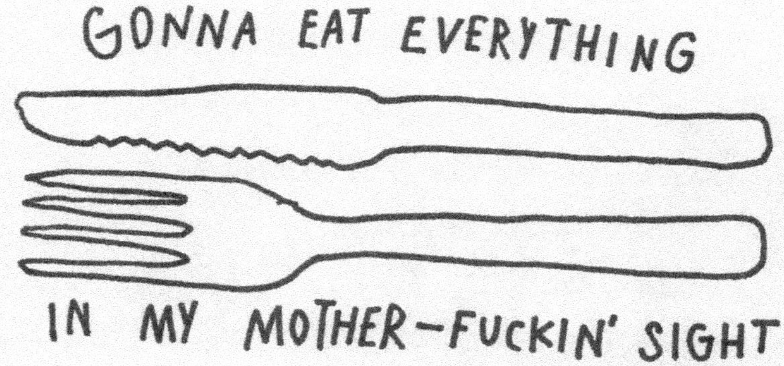

GONNA EAT EVERYTHING
IN MY MOTHER-FUCKIN' SIGHT

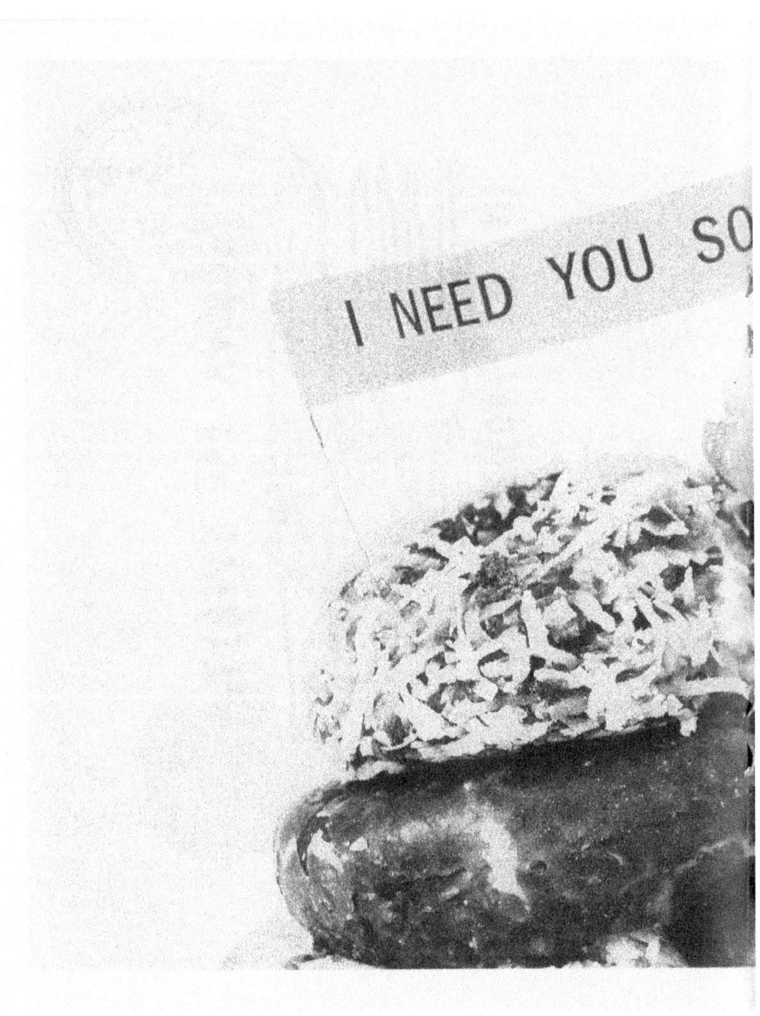

HOME BREW

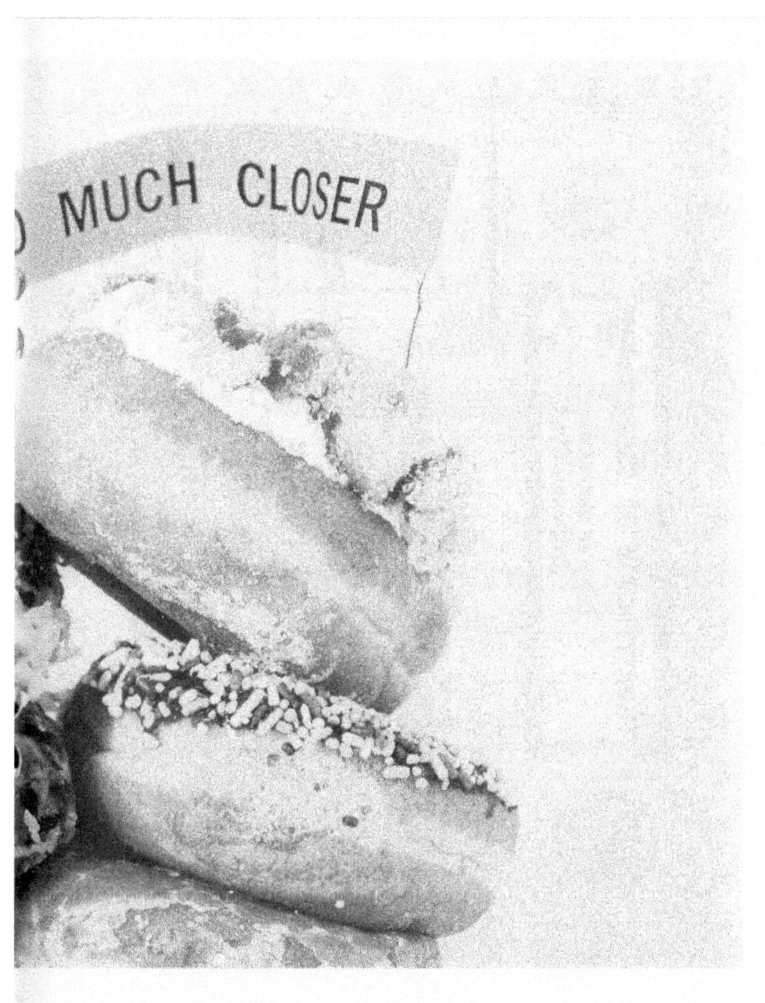
MUCH CLOSER

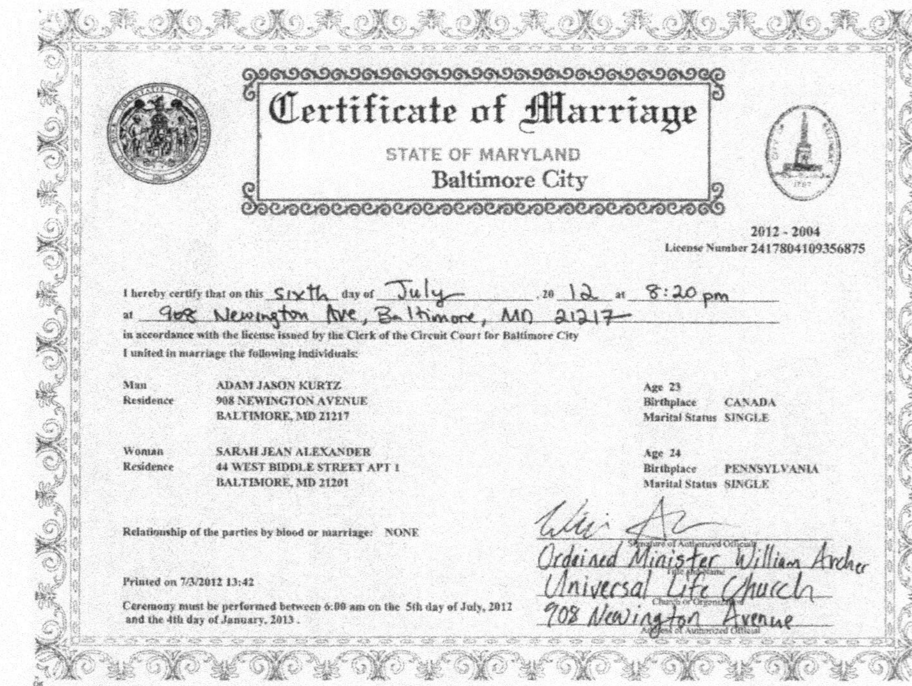

Certificate of Marriage
STATE OF MARYLAND
Baltimore City
2012 - 2004
License Number 24178041093568754
I hereby certify that on this Sixth day of July, 20 12 at 8:20 pm
at 908 Newington Ave, Baltimore, MD 21217
in accordance with the license issued by the Clerk of the Circuit Court for Baltimore City
I united in marriage the following individuals:
Man ADAM JASON KURTZ
Residence 908 NEWINGTON AVENUE
BALTIMORE, MD 21217
Age 23
Birthplace CANADA
Marital Status SINGLE
Woman SARAH JEAN ALEXANDER
Residence 44 WEST BIDDLE STREET APT 1
BALTIMORE, MD 21201
Age 24
Birthplace PENNSYLVANIA
Marital Status SINGLE
Relationship of the parties by blood or marriage: NONE
Printed on 7/3/2012 13:42
Ceremony must be performed between 6:00 am on the 5th day of July, 2012 and the 4th day of January, 2013.
Signature of Authorized Official
Ordained Minister William Archer
Title (please print)
Universal Life Church
Church of Organization
908 Newington Avenue
Address of Authorized Official

HOME BREW

6031B
Aerial view ...n – New York City.

MANHATTAN
POSTCARDS, INC.
New York, NY 10004

Tel. 212-260-5600   ManhattanPostcards.com   Printed in Singapore

SARAH JEAN' ALEXANDER

44 W. BIDDLE ST APT #1

BALTIMORE, MD 21201

THAT IS SOME SWEET SHIT

HOME BREW

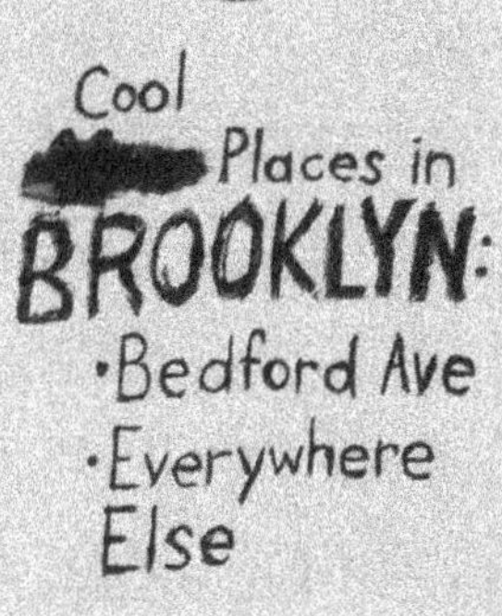
Cool
Places in
BROOKLYN:
·Bedford Ave
·Everywhere
Else

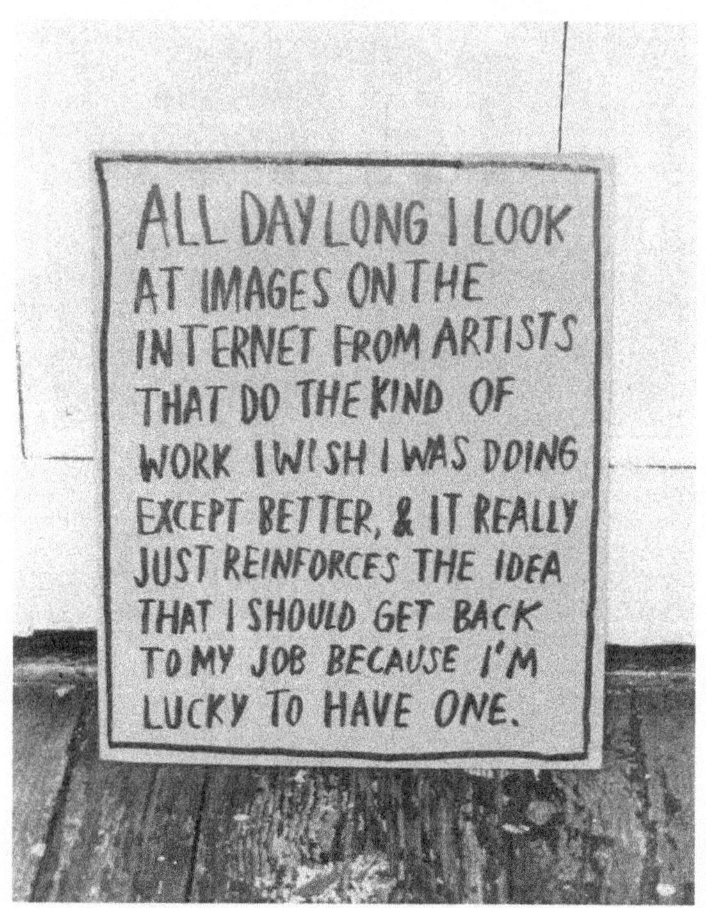

ALL DAY LONG I LOOK
AT IMAGES ON THE
INTERNET FROM ARTISTS
THAT DO THE KIND OF
WORK I WISH I WAS DOING
EXCEPT BETTER, & IT REALLY
JUST REINFORCES THE IDEA
THAT I SHOULD GET BACK
TO MY JOB BECAUSE I'M
LUCKY TO HAVE ONE.

HOME BREW

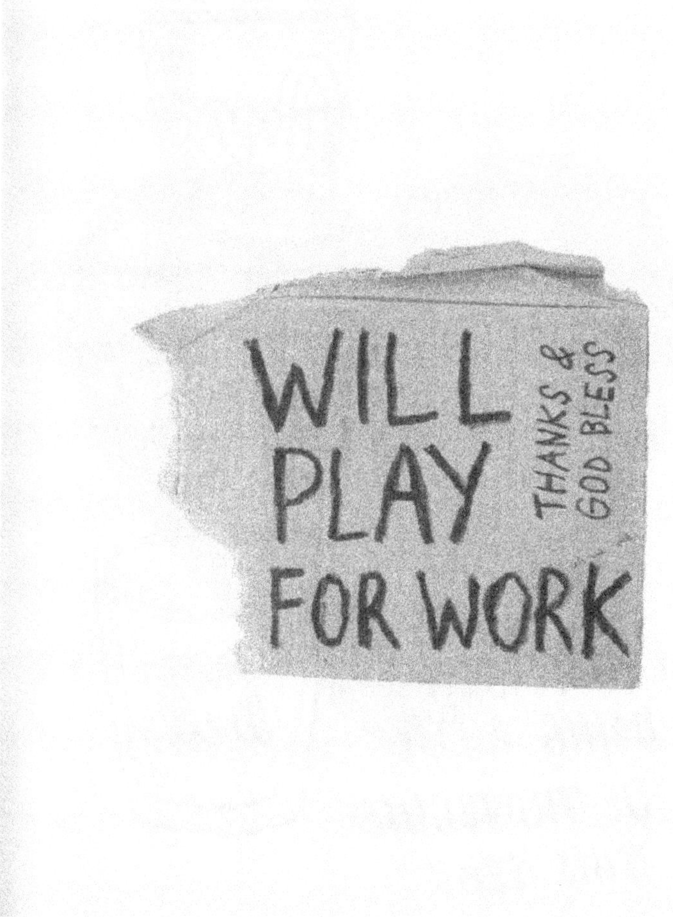

WILL
PLAY
FOR WORK
THANKS &
GOD BLESS

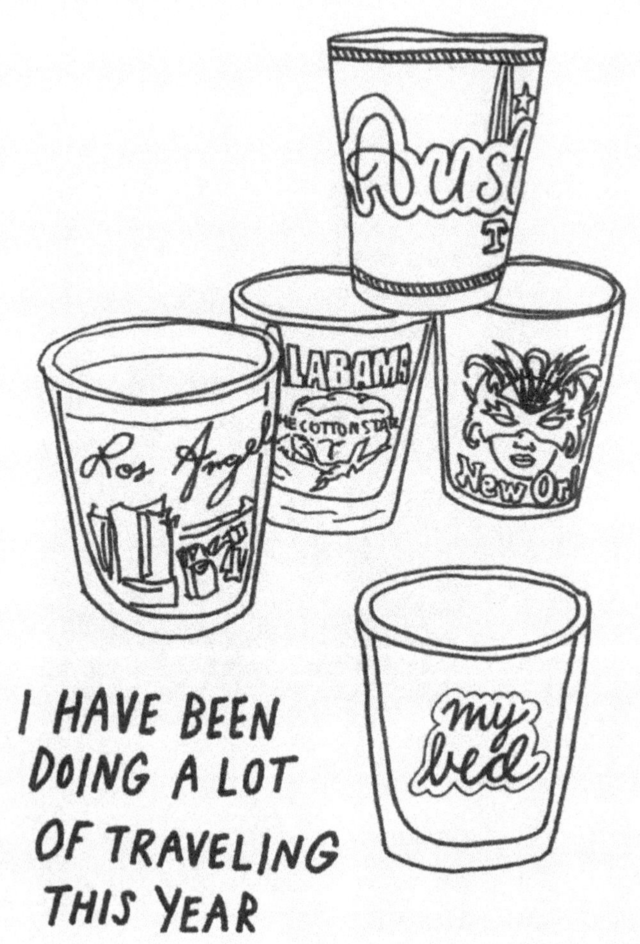

HOME BREW

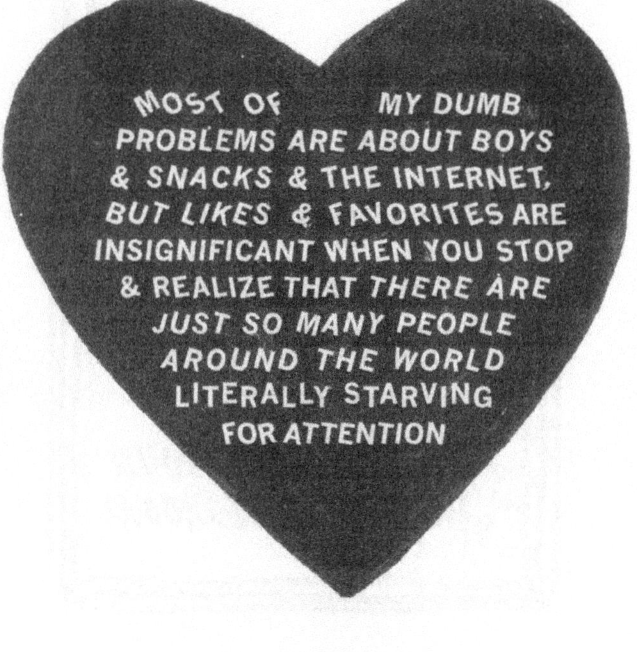

MOST OF   MY DUMB
PROBLEMS ARE ABOUT BOYS
& SNACKS & THE INTERNET,
BUT LIKES & FAVORITES ARE
INSIGNIFICANT WHEN YOU STOP
& REALIZE THAT THERE ARE
JUST SO MANY PEOPLE
AROUND THE WORLD
LITERALLY STARVING
FOR ATTENTION

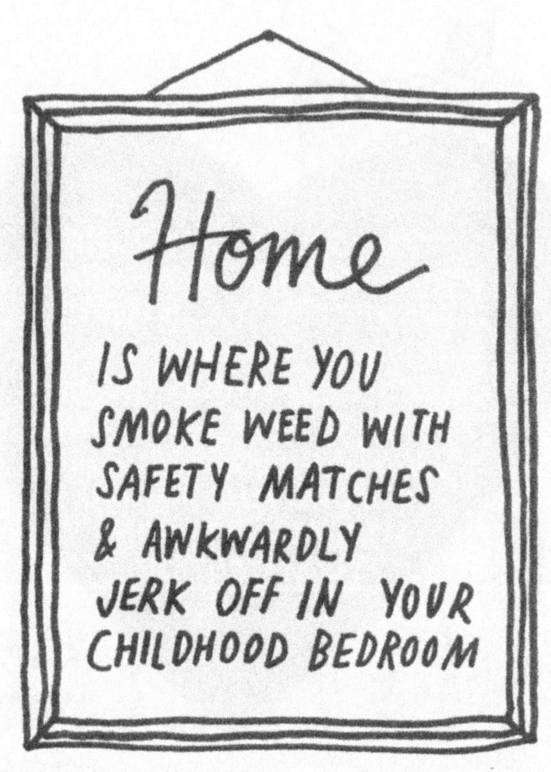
Home
IS WHERE YOU
SMOKE WEED WITH
SAFETY MATCHES
& AWKWARDLY
JERK OFF IN YOUR
CHILDHOOD BEDROOM

HOME BREW

DON'T TALK TO ME
I AM TRYING
TO REMEMBER
WHAT YOU JUST
SAID SO I CAN
TWEET IT

THAT'S IT
GO HOME
~~I AM TIRED~~
~~NOW~~

HOME BREW

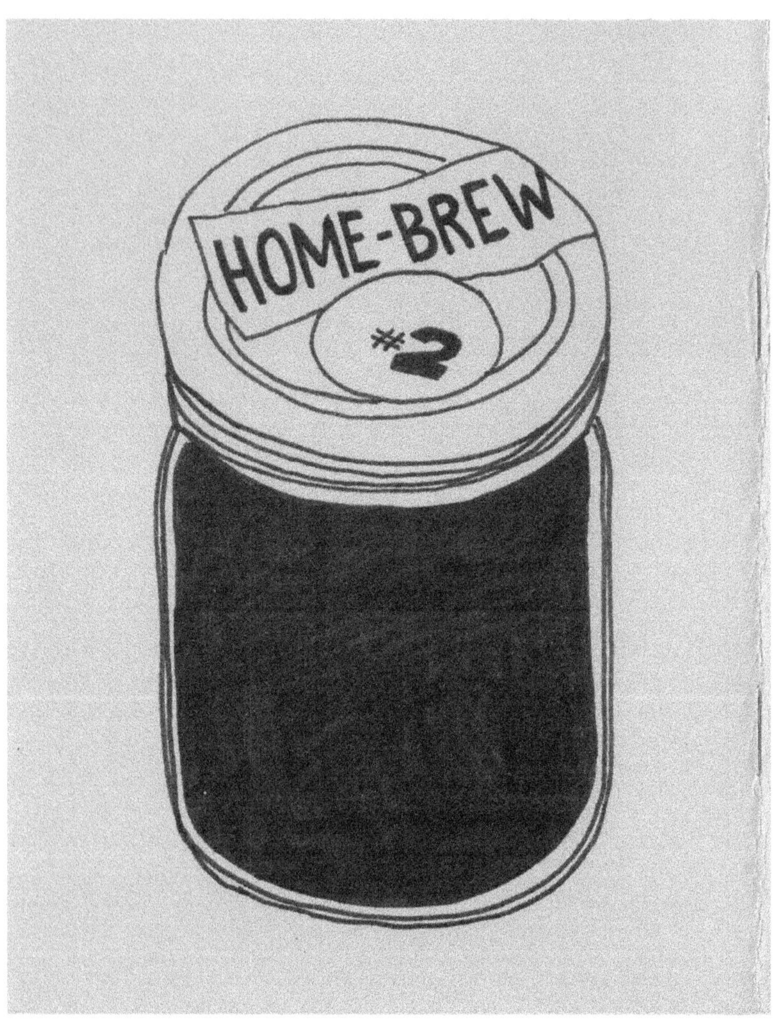

HOME BREW

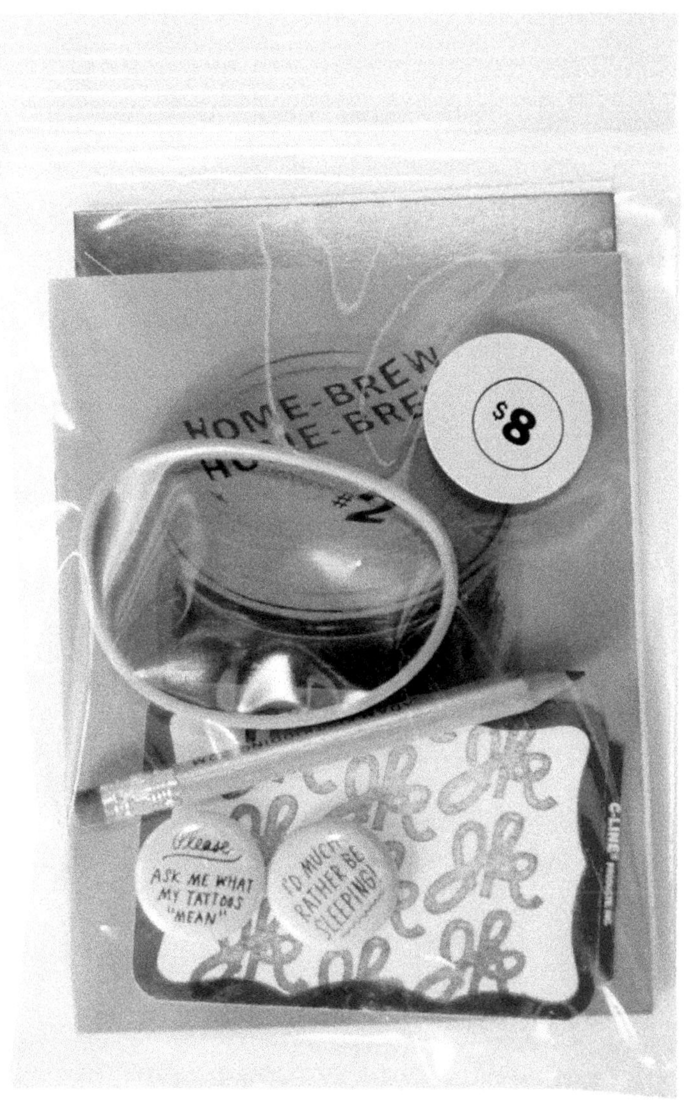
HOME-BREW
HOME-BREW
#2
$8
Please
ASK ME WHAT
MY TATTOOS
"MEAN"
I'D MUCH
RATHER BE
SLEEPING!

HOME BREW

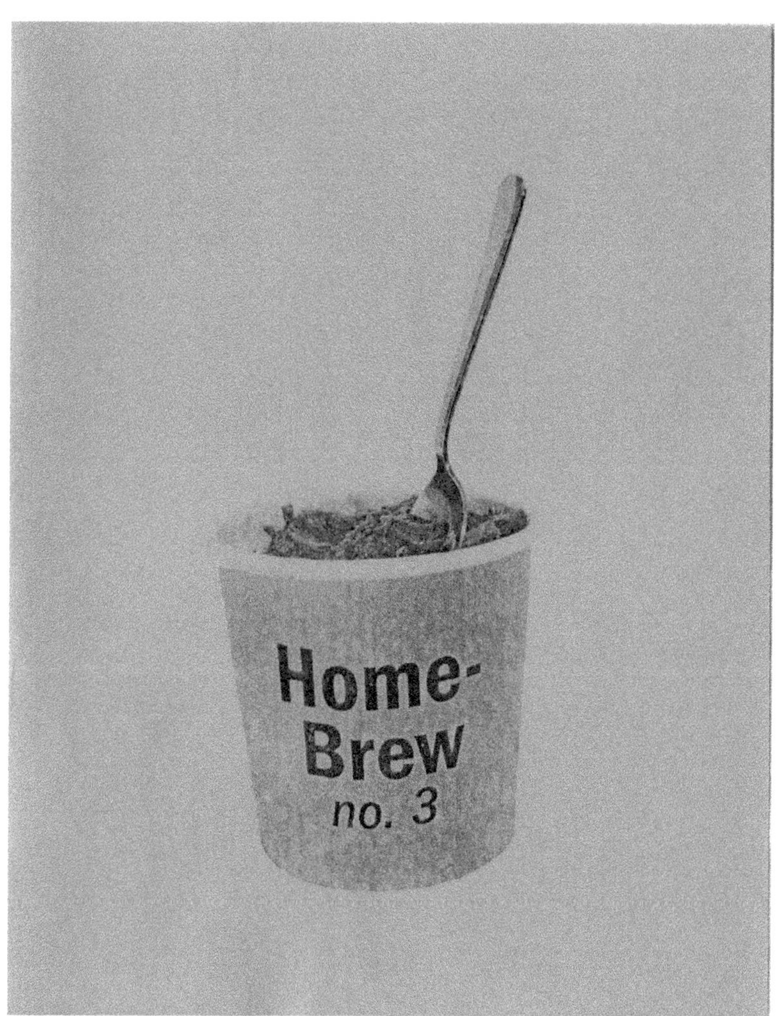
Home-
Brew
no. 3

04/25/13

MITCHELL,

SOME DAYS I STILL DON'T
UNDERSTAND WHY YOU
EVEN LOVE ME. OTHER
DAYS I DON'T CARE
BECAUSE I KNOW YOU DO
& THAT'S ALL THAT
MATTERS.

I AM NOT THAT SPECIAL
& NEITHER IS THIS ZINE
BUT I AM HAPPY YOU
WANT US BOTH.

                        -Adam

HOME BREW

STILL MORE MOODS, MESS, & MISTAKES REGARDING PEOPLE, PLACES, & THINGS

by

ADAM J. KURTZ

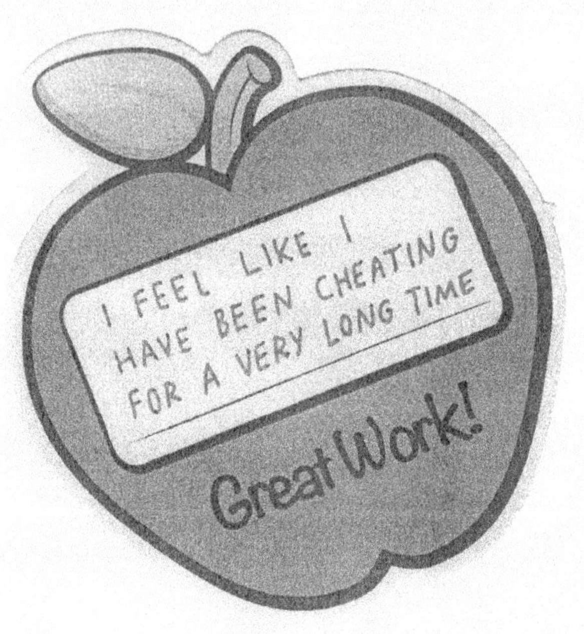

I FEEL LIKE I HAVE BEEN CHEATING FOR A VERY LONG TIME
Great Work!

HOME BREW

Dear Mom,

I had this weird "aha" moment the other night, and suddenly everything started to

CLICK TO CONTINUE

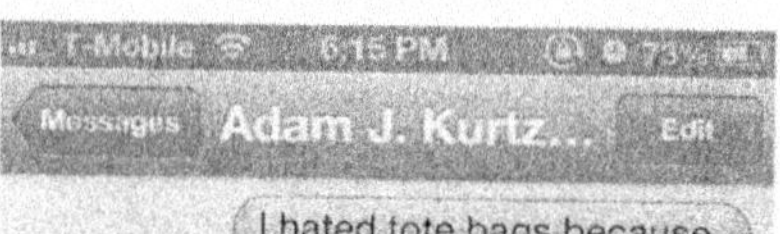
T-Mobile 6:15 PM 73%
Messages Adam J. Kurtz... Edit
I hated tote bags because I didn't understand potential but aesthetics meaning story travel exclusivity attachment and practical use in time of need made me love it. I can make tools that help people realize they are the tool. inspire everyone.
I hated tote bags because I didn't understand potential but aesthetics meaning story travel exclusivity attachment and practical use in time of need made me love it. I can make tools that help people realize they are the tool. inspire everyone.

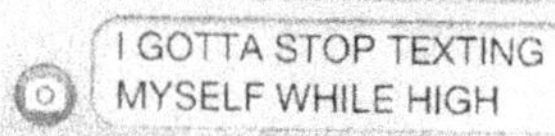
I GOTTA STOP TEXTING MYSELF WHILE HIGH

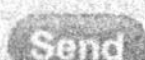
Send

HOME BREW

WIN A <u>FREE</u> IPHONE!

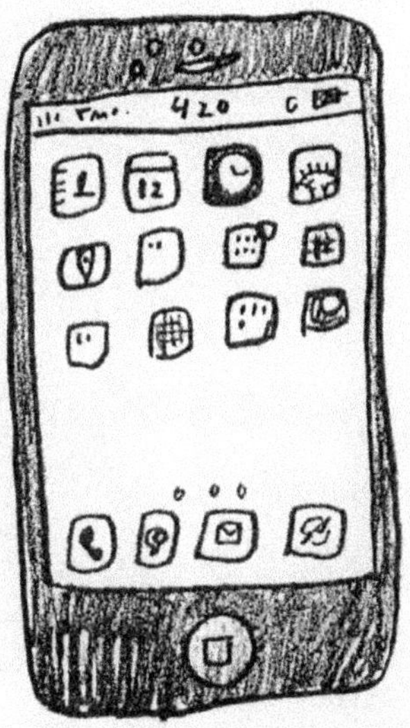

I CAN'T HANDLE
IT ANYMORE!

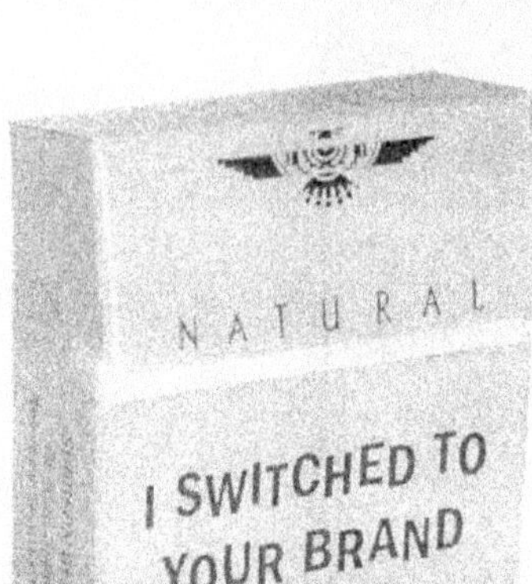

NATURAL
I SWITCHED TO
YOUR BRAND
TO FEEL
CLOSER TO YOU
& I'M SORRY

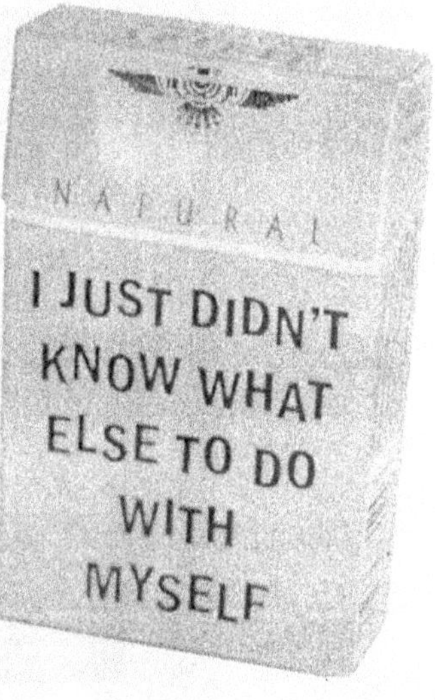

NATURAL
I JUST DIDN'T
KNOW WHAT
ELSE TO DO
WITH
MYSELF

HOME BREW

PROPOSED MANTRAS

"IT'S TOO BAD 'COOL' IS A SOCIAL CONSTRUCT BECAUSE I AM PRETTY COOL"

"~~IF AT FIRST YOU DON'T SUCCEED~~"

"NOTHING MATTERS, EAT CHIPS"

"I CAN DO ANYTHING IF I JUST PUT IT TO MY FOREHEAD & APPLY PRESSURE"

"I AM DEFINITELY WORTH REBLOGGING"

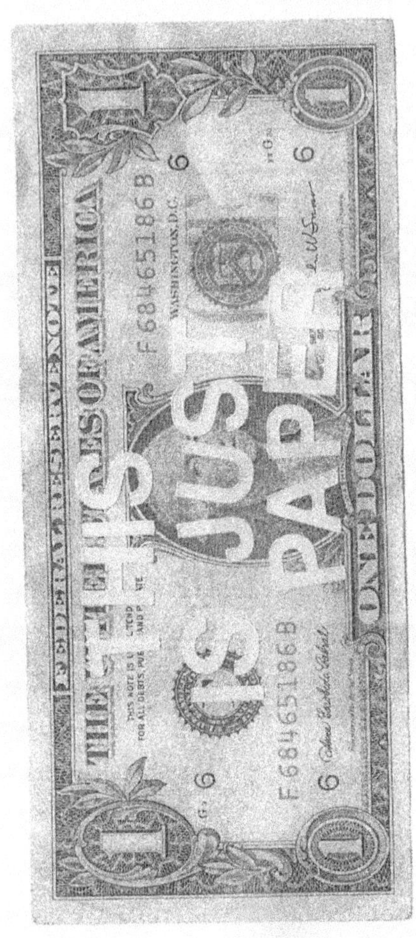

HOME BREW

ROCK BEATS
SCISSORS,
BUT
PAPER WINS
EVERY TIME

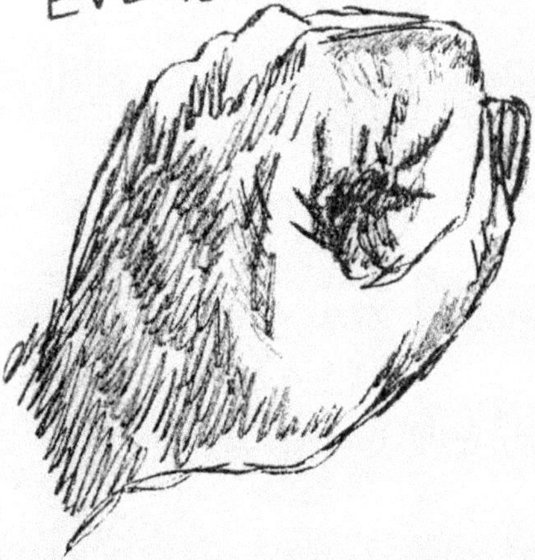

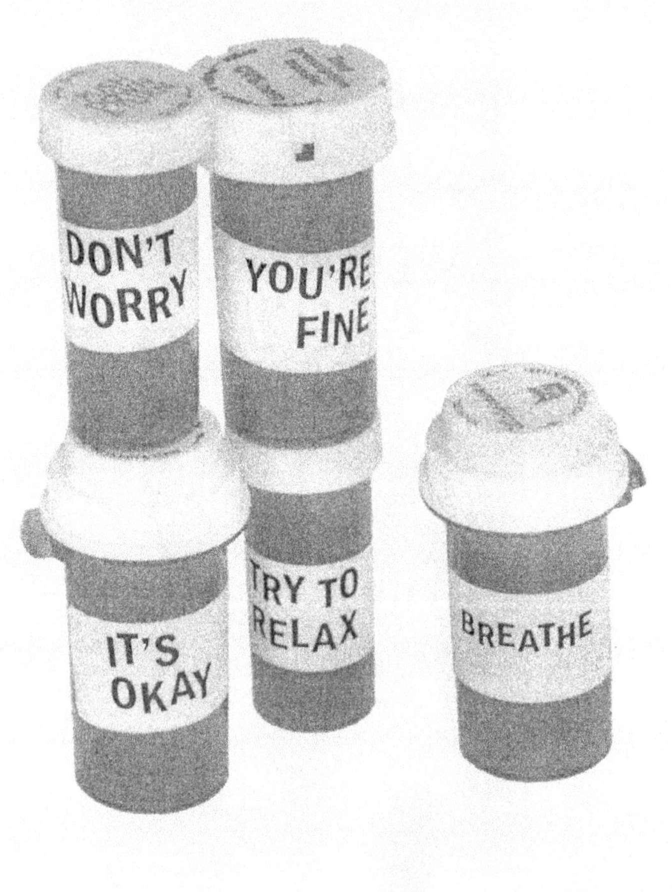

HOME BREW

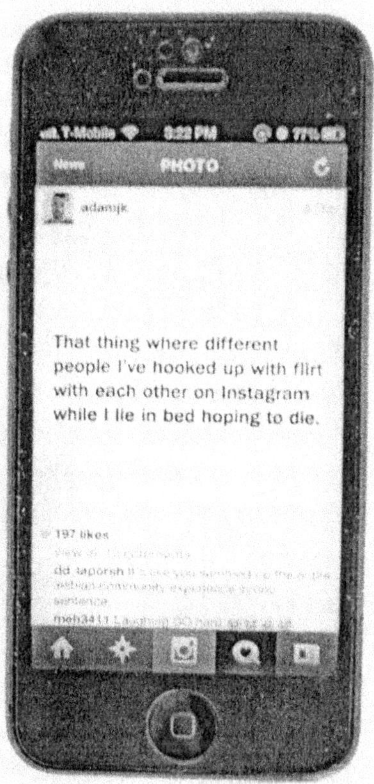
PHOTO
adamjk
That thing where different people I've hooked up with flirt with each other on Instagram while I lie in bed hoping to die.
197 likes

SORRY I AM SUCH AN ASSHOLE
SORRY I AM NOT ENOUGH OF ONE
SORRY I SAID 1 THING & DID ANOTHER
SORRY I AM NOT AS EMOTIONALLY
 STABLE AS I WOULD LIKE TO BE
SORRY I CAN'T SEEM TO PRIORITIZE
THINGS THAT MATTER
SORRY I TALK SO MUCH ABOUT THINGS
 YOU DON'T CARE ABOUT
SORRY I DON'T LIKE DRINKING MUCH
SORRY I FEEL WEIRD SOCIAL
 PRESSURES THAT DON'T EXIST
SORRY I MADE YOU FEEL LESS
 THAN WANTED
 SORRY I WAS QUIET THAT 1 TIME
SORRY YOU DON'T LIKE THAT THING
 THAT I ACTUALLY LOVE
SORRY I AM SO BUSY PRETENDING
 TO BE BUSY

SORRY I HAVE SO LITTLE SELF CONTROL
SORRY I NEVER VOCALIZED MY INTENT
SORRY I STOLE AS A CHILD
SORRY I START THEN STOP THEN
START THEN STOP AGA
SORRY I CREATE UNNECESSARILY
COMPLICATED SITUATIONS ALL THE TIME
SORRY I FALL IN LOVE WITH PEOPLE
WHO AREN'T YOU
SORRY I AM SUCH A FAST LEARNER
& A SLOW UNLEARNER
SORRY I KEEP SAYING SORRY AND
MEANING IT SINCERELY
SORRY I RELY ON YOU AS MUCH AS I DO
SORRY I TALK DURING SEX EVEN
THOUGH YOU HATE THAT
SORRY I CAN'T REALLY FOCUS ON
THE THINGS YOU NEED ME TO FOCUS ON
SORRY I GIVE FALSE SIGNIFICANCE
TO TINY DETAILS & SITUATIONS

I DIDN'T KNOW THAT
LOVE SONGS ARE REAL
& NOW I CAN'T STOP
HEARING THEM & IT'S
ALL YOUR FAULT

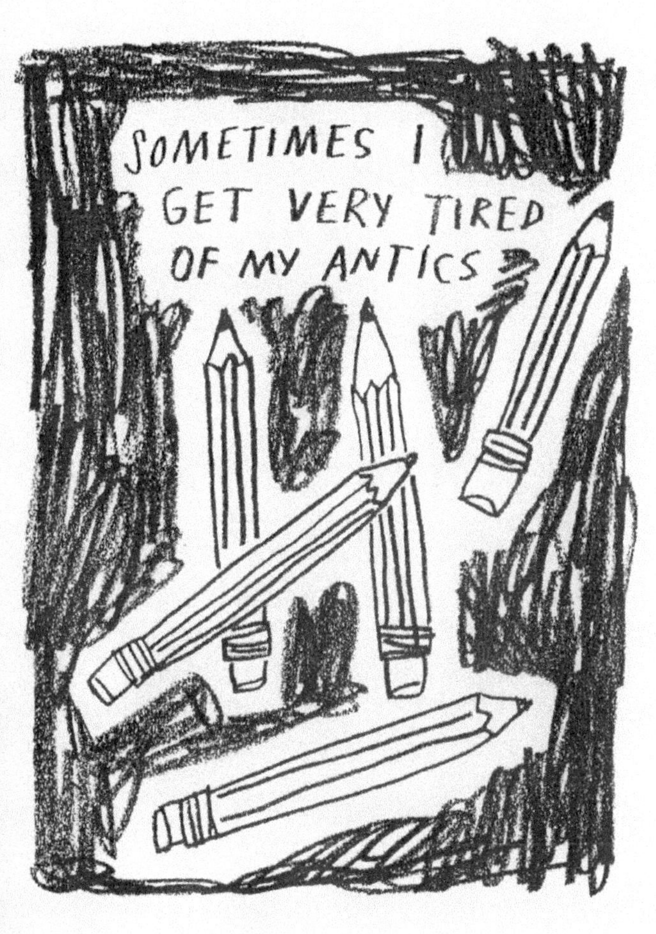

SOMETIMES I
GET VERY TIRED
OF MY ANTICS

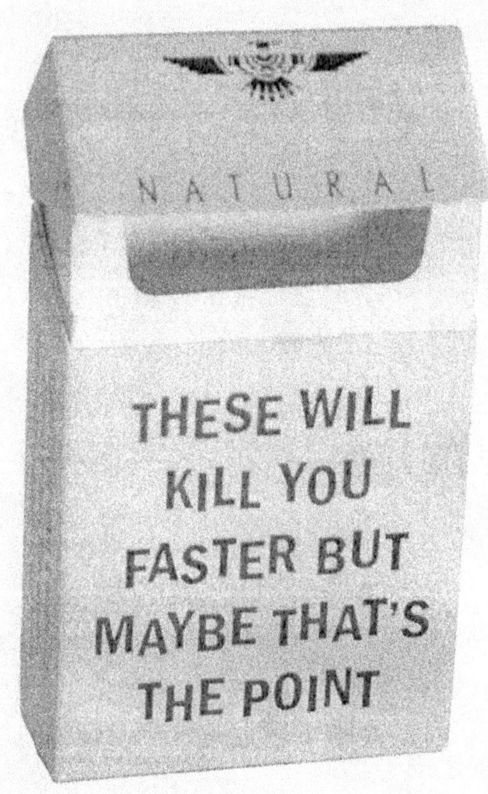
NATURAL
THESE WILL
KILL YOU
FASTER BUT
MAYBE THAT'S
THE POINT

HOME BREW

i'm not afraid because i'm letting you in,

i'm afraid because i'm gradually giving you the power to destroy me completely

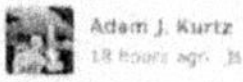

I look at your endless stream
of perfect snapshots and I
imagine myself living the
wonderful relationship we
never would have had anyway.

HOME BREW

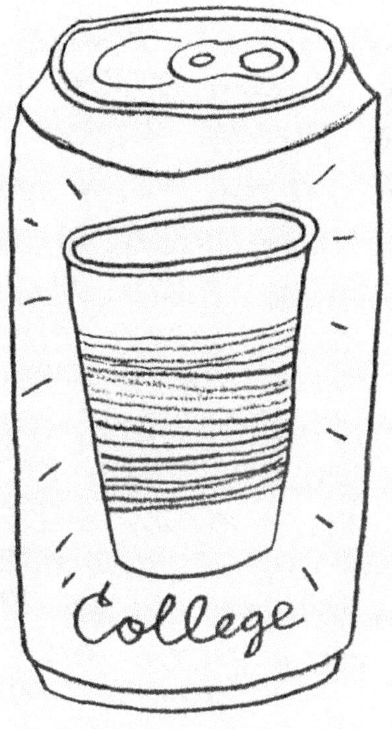
College

PIZZA PIZZA PIZZA PIZZA
PIZZA PIZZA PIZZA PIZZA
PIZZA PIZZA PIZZA PIZZA
PIZZA PIZZA PIZZA PIZZA
PIZZA PIZZA PIZZA PIZZA
PIZZA PIZZA PIZZA PIZZA
PIZZA PIZZA PIZZA PIZZA
PIZZA PIZZA PIZZA PIZZA
PIZZA PIZZA PIZZA PIZZA
PIZZA PIZZA PIZZA PIZZA
PIZZA PIZZA PIZZA PIZZA
PIZZA PIZZA PIZZA PIZZA
PIZZA PIZZA PIZZA PIZZA
PIZZA PIZZA PIZZA PIZZA
PIZZA PIZZA PIZZA PIZZA
PIZZA PIZZA PIZZA
PIZZA PIZZA

CALM DOWN,
IT'S OK, YOU'RE
NOT AN ARTIST
YOU JUST HAVE
A BLOG.

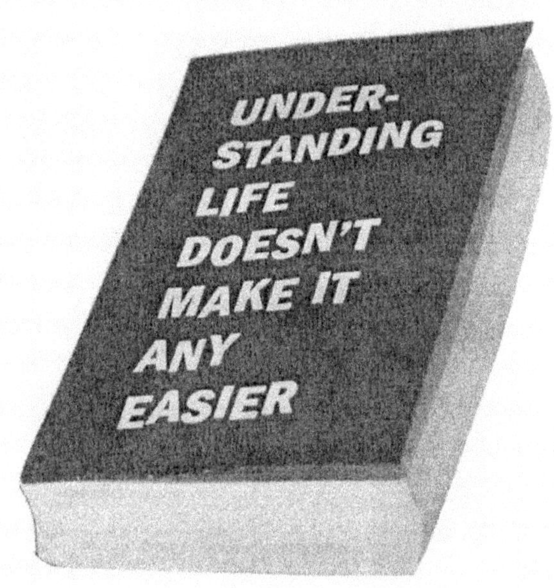

HOME BREW

1. START BY HOLDING DOWN THE SLEEP/WAKE BUTTON AT THE TOP RIGHT-HAND CORNER OF THE IPHONE FOR A FEW SECONDS

2. THIS WILL BRING UP A SCREEN ASKING YOU TO RUN THE SLIDER ACROSS THE SCREEN TO TURN OFF THE IPHONE

3. IF YOU DON'T WANT TO DO THIS, JUST TAP THE CANCEL BUTTON AT THE BOTTOM OF THE SCREEN

4. IF YOU DO, THOUGH, MOVE THE SLIDER TO THE RIGHT. WHEN YOU DO, A PROGRESS WHEEL WILL APPEAR AND IN A SECOND OR TWO THE IPHONE WILL TURN OFF

5. TO TURN IT BACK ON AGAIN, JUST HOLD DOWN THE SLEEP/WAKE BUTTON AGAIN UNTIL THE APPLE ICON APPEARS ON THE SCREEN

6. THEN LET THE BUTTON GO AND THEN WAIT FOR THE PHONE TO START UP

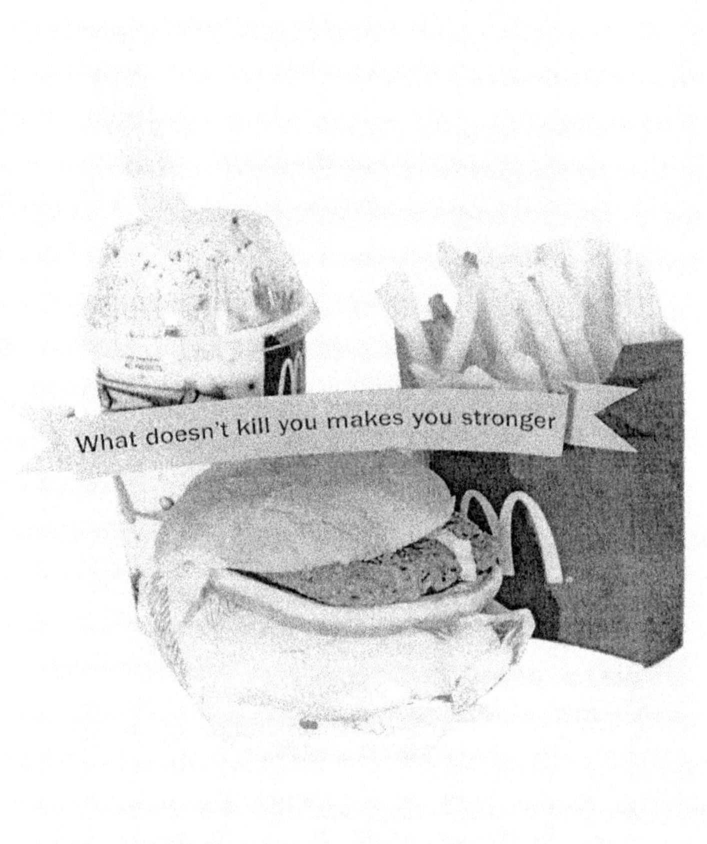

HOME BREW

ADAMJK.COM

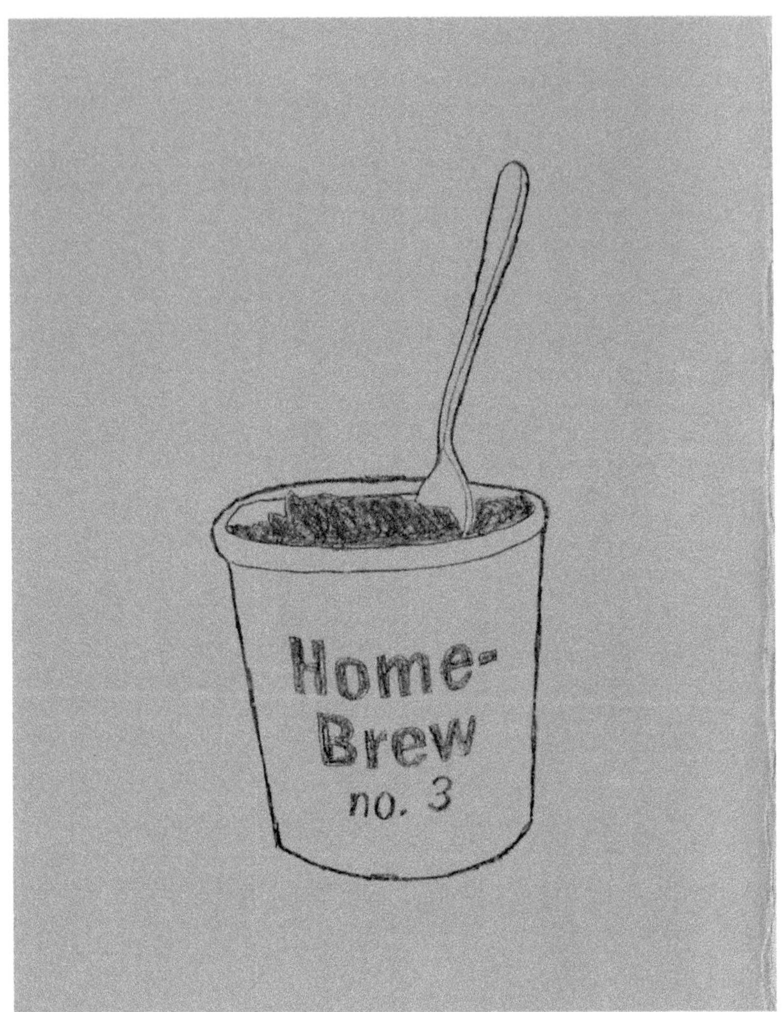

HOME BREW

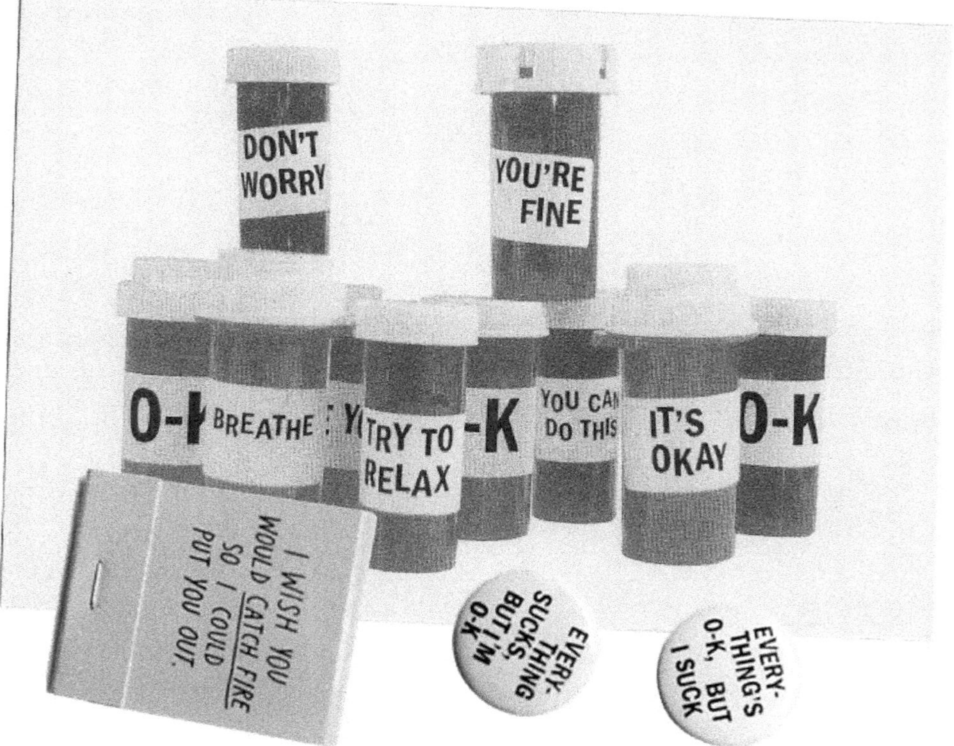
DON'T
WORRY
YOU'RE
FINE
O-K
BREATHE
TRY TO
RELAX
O-K
YOU CAN
DO THIS
IT'S
OKAY
O-K
I WISH YOU
WOULD CATCH FIRE
SO I COULD
PUT YOU OUT.
EVERY-
THING
SUCKS,
BUT I'M
O-K
EVERY-
THING'S
O-K, BUT
I SUCK

HOME BREW

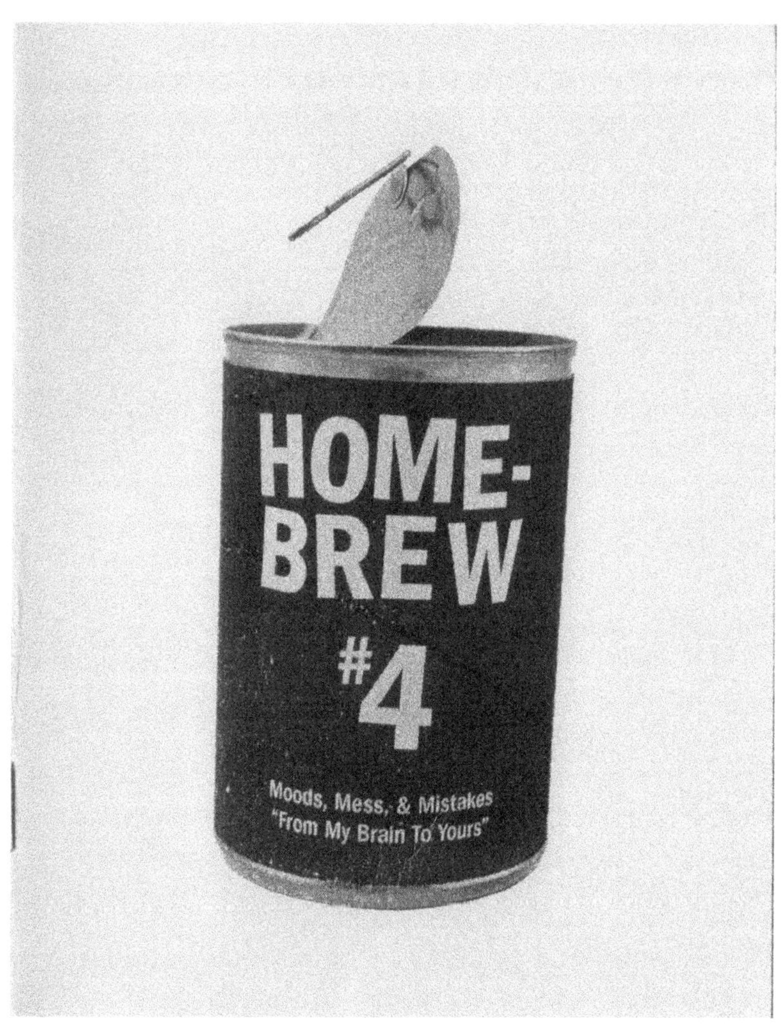

HOME-
BREW
#4
Moods, Mess, & Mistakes
"From My Brain To Yours"

HOME BREW

YES, O-K, SURE, HERE'S
MORE MOODS, MESS,
& MISTAKES, FROM
MY BRAIN TO YOURS.

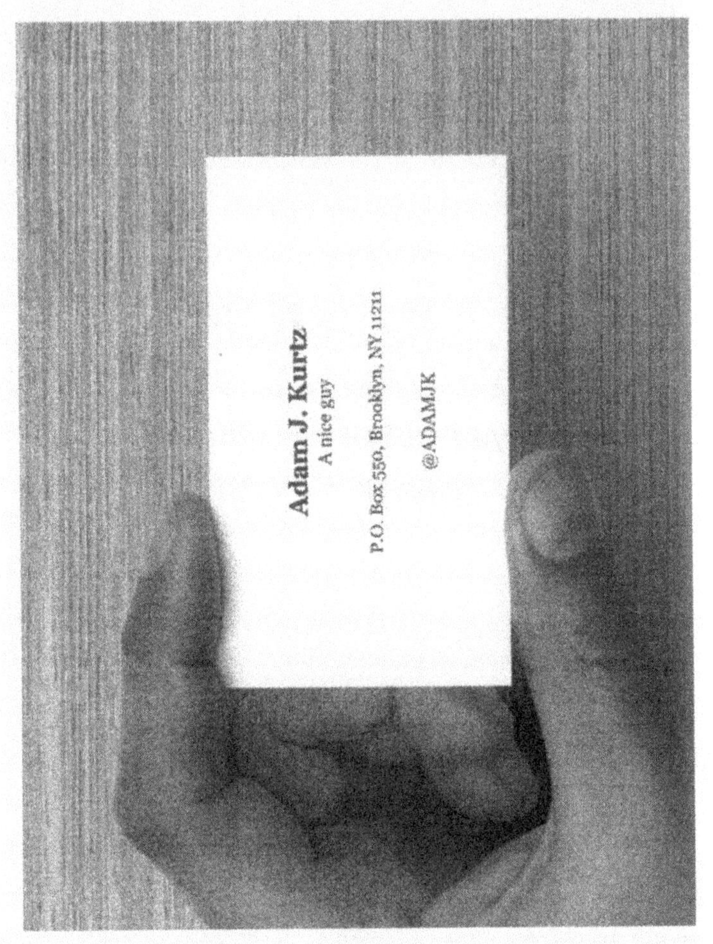

HOME BREW

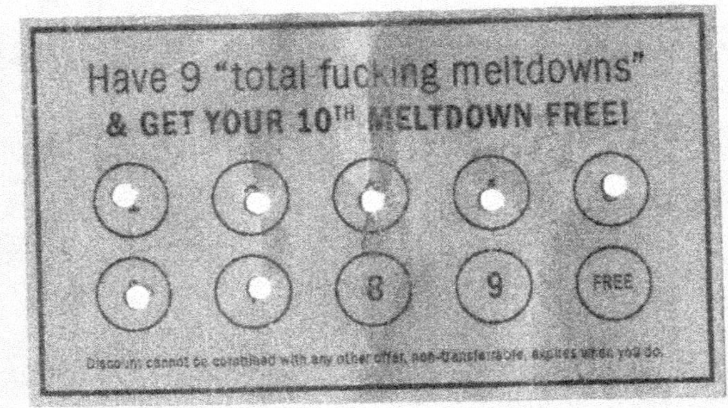

Have 9 "total fucking meltdowns"
& GET YOUR 10TH MELTDOWN FREE!
8
9
FREE
Discount cannot be combined with any other offer, non-transferable, expires when you do.

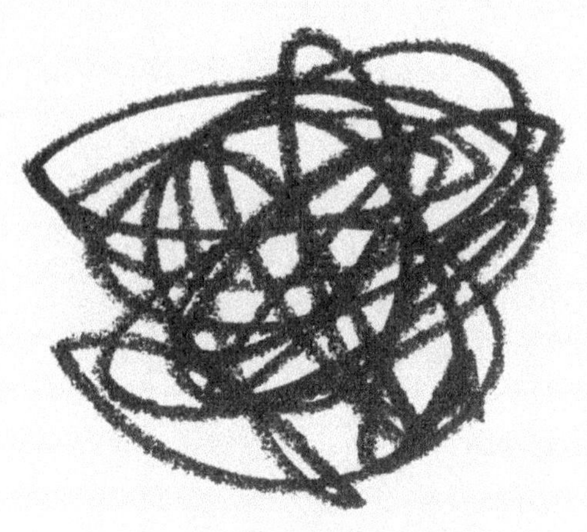

Sometimes I THINK
ABOUT ALL THE
terrible shit THAT
IS HAPPENING IN
THE WORLD & OTHER
TIMES I'M distracting
MYSELF.

HOME BREW

don't give me your number
just give me your wifi
password

don't give me your number
just give me your wifi
password

don't give me your number
just give me your wifi
password

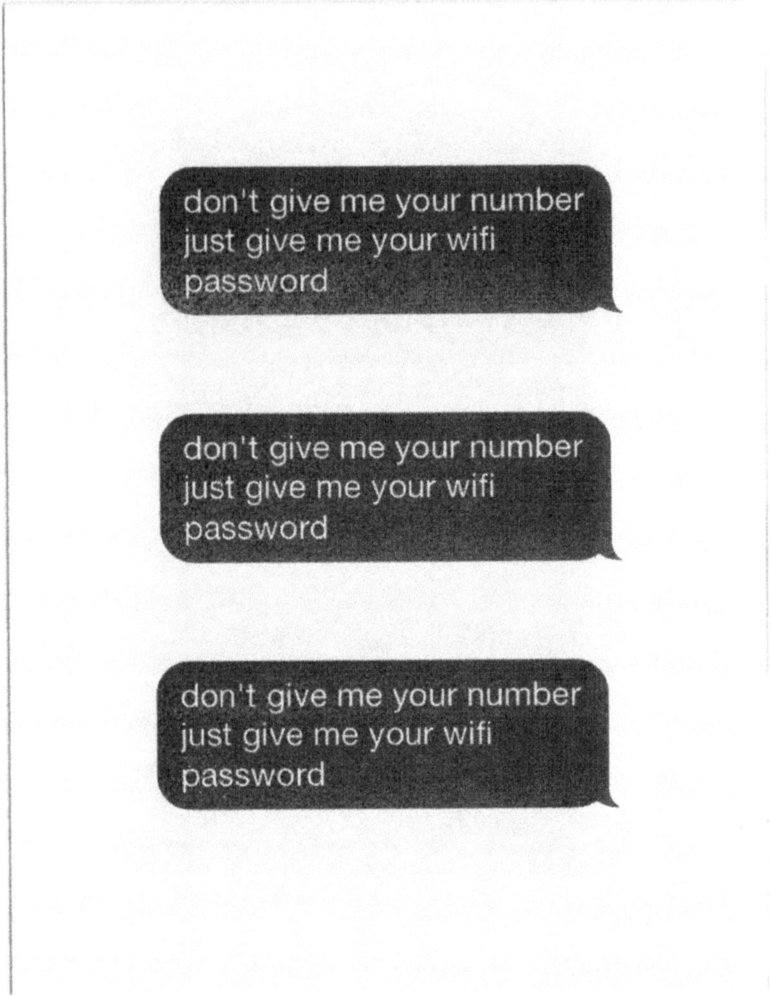

HOME BREW

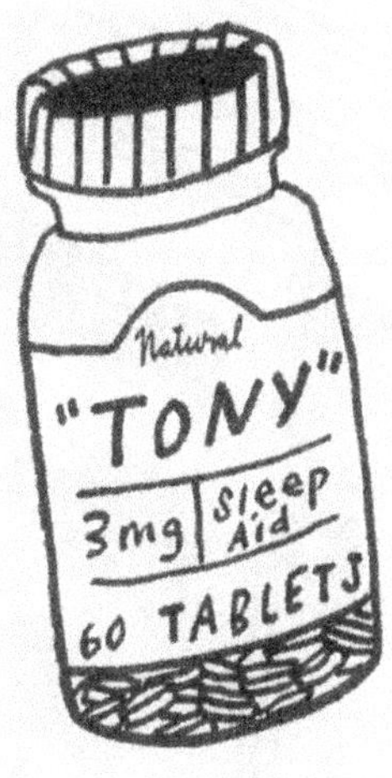

I JUST CAN'T SLEEP
WITHOUT YOU, BABE.

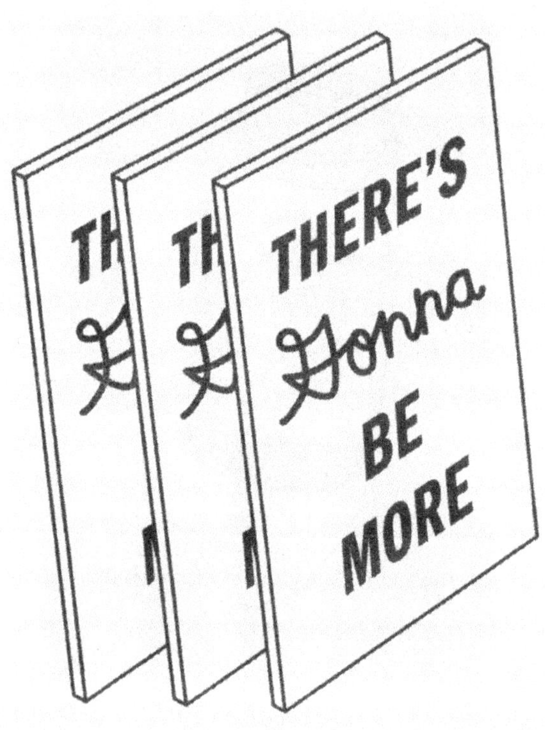

HOME BREW

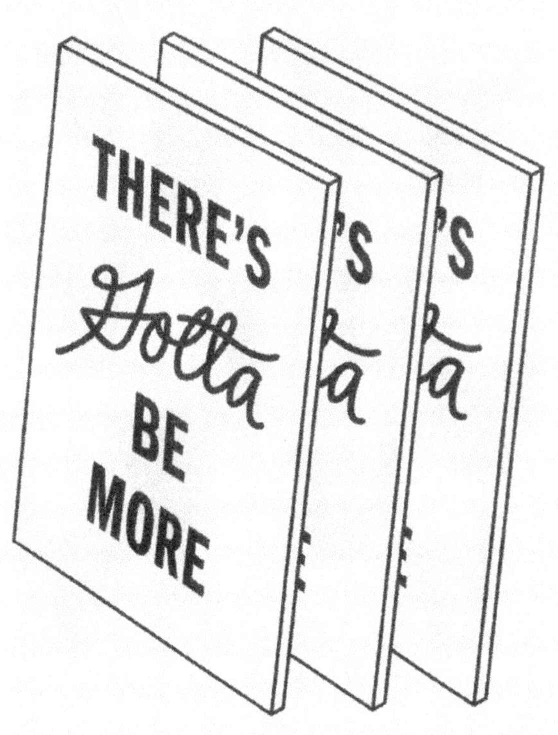

THERE'S
Gotta
BE
MORE

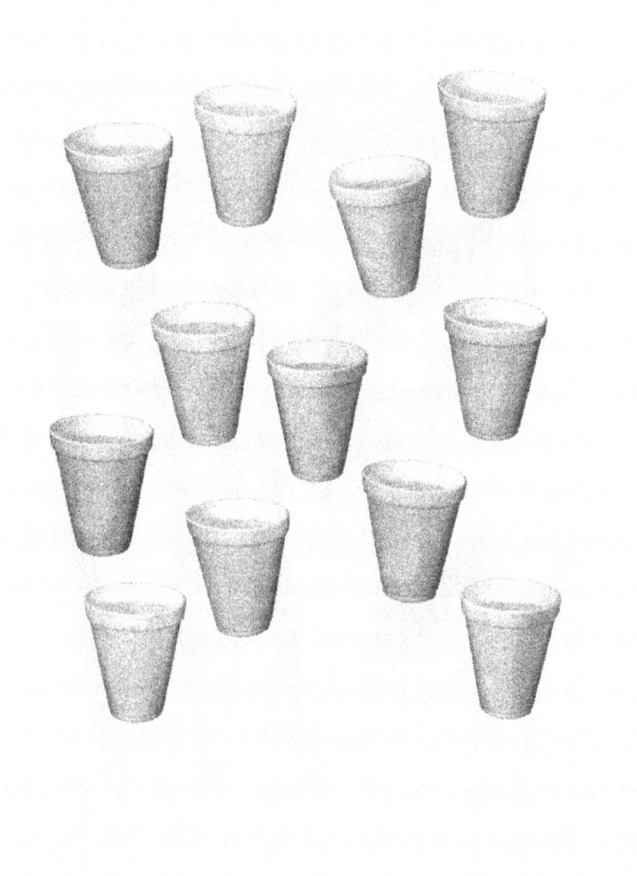

HOME BREW

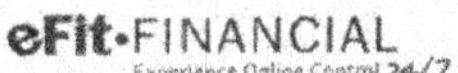

04/15/2014

P.O. Box 27272
Denver, CO 80227

Friendly Payment Reminder

This notice is to remind you that your payment is past due

adam kurtz
276 south 5th st apt3
bk, NY 11211

RE: Green Fitness Studio
Account#1216509

Amount Due :$0.01

For Customer Service Please Call (866) 462-3348

Return This Portion With Your Payment

Send to: **eFit Financial** – P.O. Box 27272, Denver, CO 80227

SEND YOUR PAYMENT NOW TO AVOID FURTHER LATE CHARGES

RE: adam kurtz

Account# : 1216509

Past Due Payments:	$0.01
Late Charges:	
Return Charges:	
Amount Due Now:	**$0.01**

Please disregard this notice if you have already sent your payment, thank you.

When you provide a check as payment, you authorize us either to use the information from your check to make a one-time electronic fund transfer from your account or to process the payment as a check transaction.

All returned items will be charged a $30.00 return fee

New Address?
Please check box ☐   Member Account #1216509

Old Address

Name_______________

Address_______________

City__________ State____ Zip____

Phone Number (   )_______________

New Address

Name_______________

Address_______________

City__________ State____ Zip____

Phone Number (   )_______________

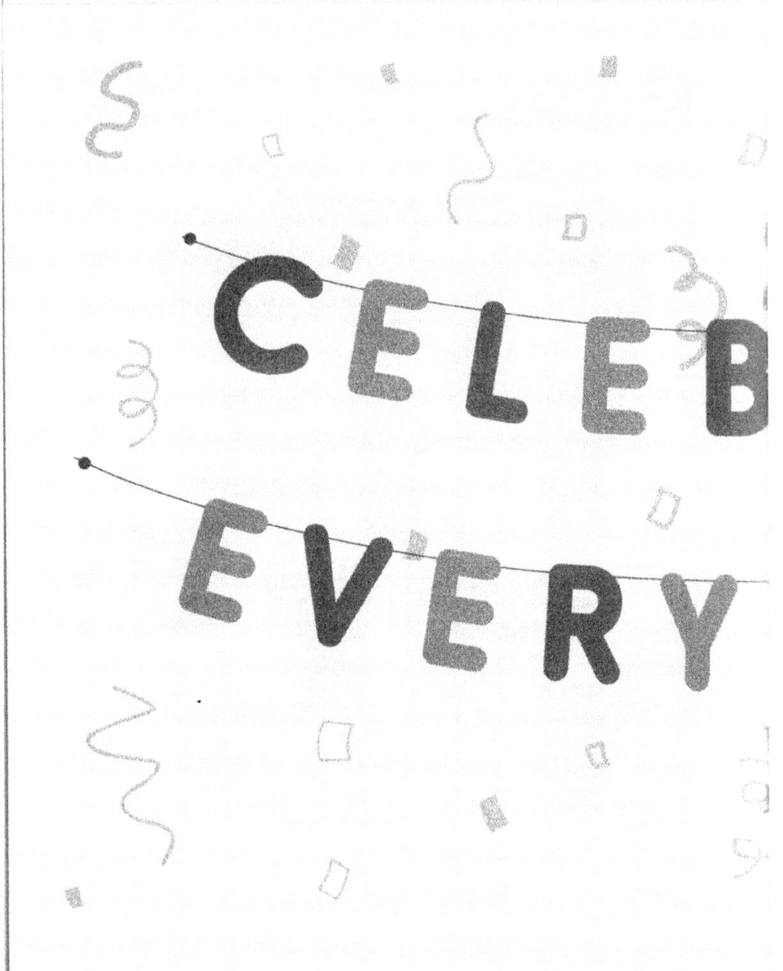

HOME BREW

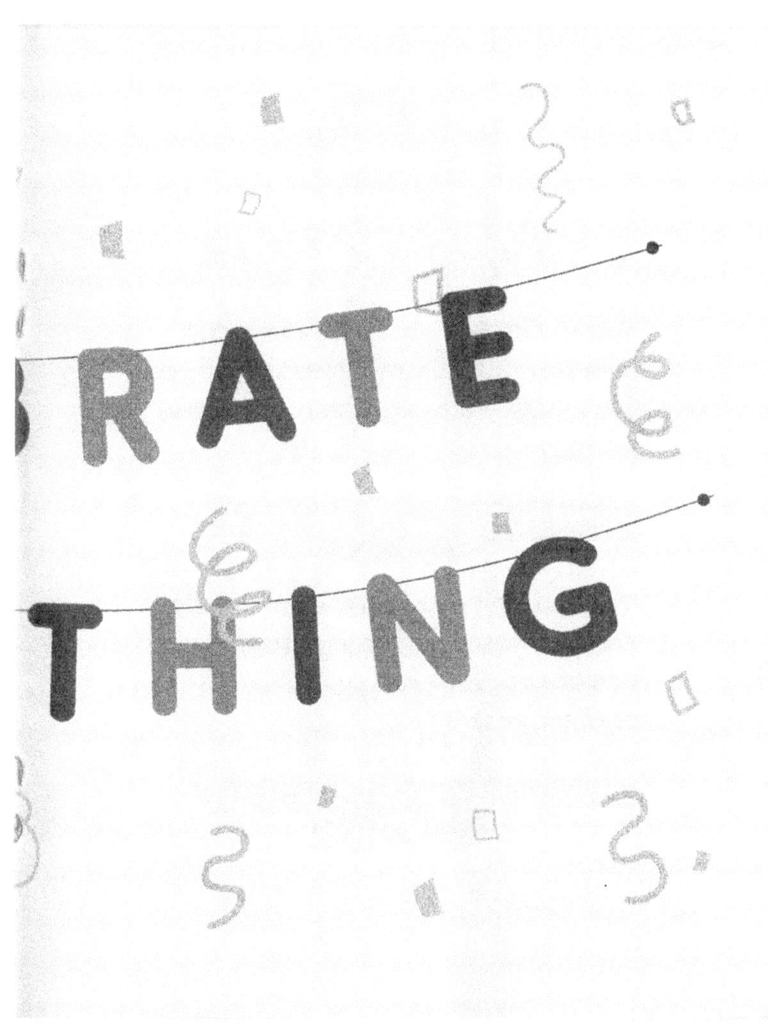

BRATE
THING

nobody knows you're freaking out
unless you tell them, especially if you
live in new york city where everyone
is crazy

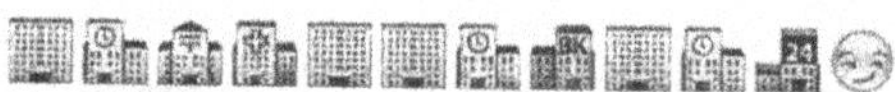

think before you speak, like literally
compile your complete thoughts and
opinions before you give them to
another person

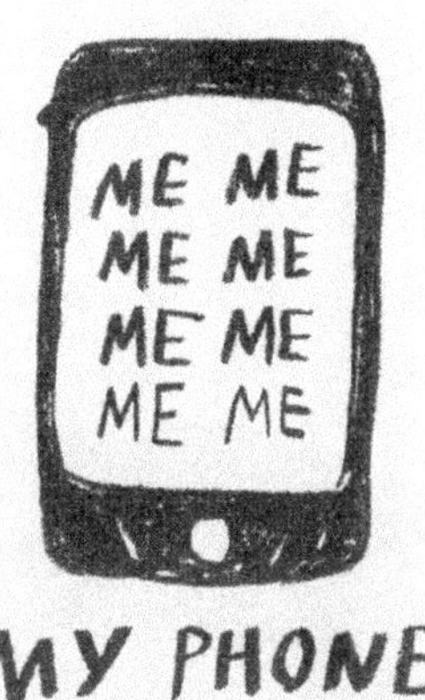

MY PHONE

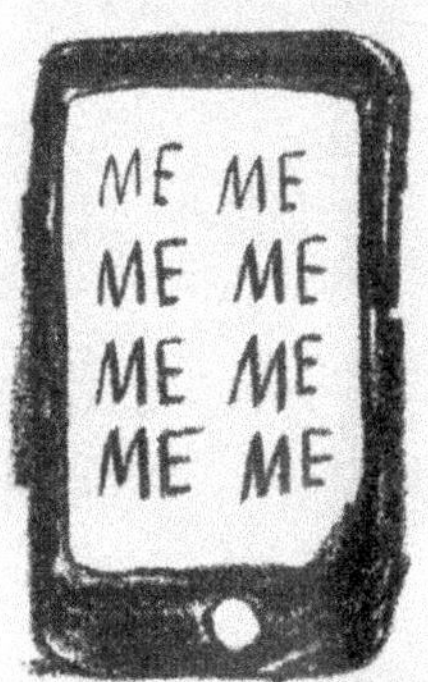

MY OTHER PHONE

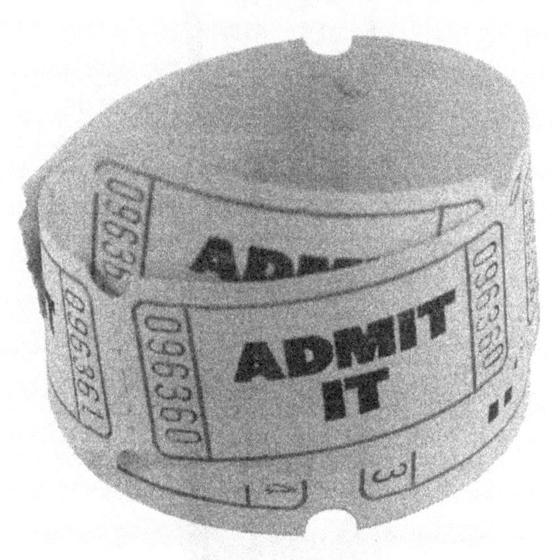

HOME BREW

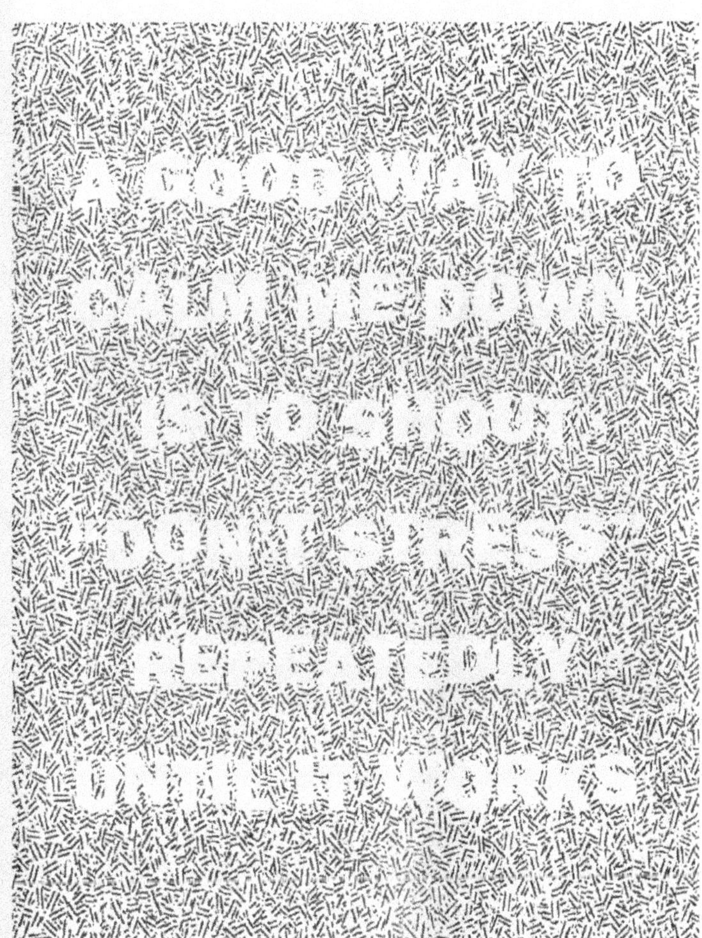
A GOOD WAY TO
CALM ME DOWN
IS TO SHOUT
DON'T STRESS
REPEATEDLY
UNTIL IT WORKS

SORRY SORRY SORRY SORRY
SORRY SORRY SORRY SORRY
SORRY SORRY SORRY
SORRY SORRY SORRY SORRY
SORRY SORRY SORRY SORRY
SORRY SORRY SORRY SORRY
SORRY SORRY SORRY
SORRY SORRY
SORRY SORRY SORRY

HOME BREW

Don't   Don't   Don't
Stress Don't Stress Don't Stress Don't
Don't Stress Don't Stress Don't Stress
Don't Stress Don't Stress Don't Stress
Stress Don't Stress Don't Stress Don't
Don't Stress Don't Stress Don't Stress Don't
Stress Don't Stress Don't Stress Don't Stress
Don't Stress Don't Stress Don't Stress Don't
Stress Don't Stress Don't Stress Don't Stress
Don't Stress Don't Stress Don't Stress
Don't Stress Don't Stress Don't Stress
Stress Don't Stress Don't Stress Don't
Don't Stress Don't Stress Don't Stress
Stress Don't Stress Don't Stress Don't
Don't Stress Don't Stress Don't Stress
Stress Don't Stress Don't Stress Don't
Don't Stress Don't Stress Don't Stress
Stress   Stress Don't Stress
          Stress

HEMORRHAGING
FOLLOWERS & FEELING
FINE: A How-To Guide
For Self-Acceptance In
The Internet Age
by
ADAM J. KURTZ
"Author of No Other Books"

HOME BREW

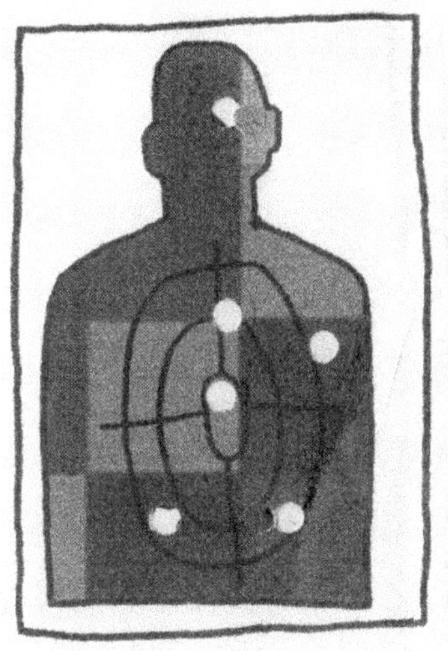 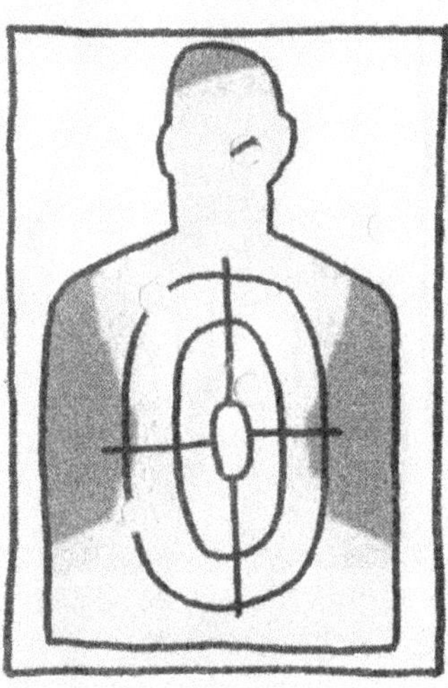

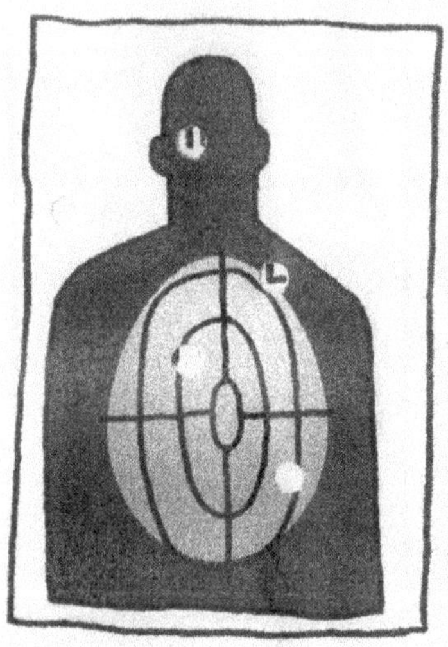 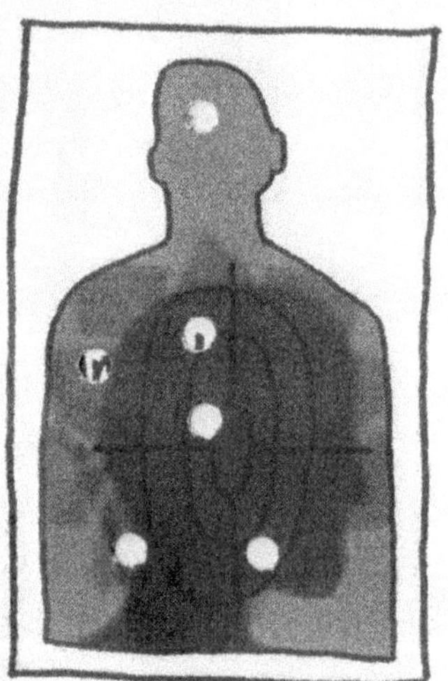

HOME BREW

I know what we did, but I can't remember what it felt like...

YES YES YES YES YES
YES YES YES YES YES
YES YES YES YES YES YES
YES YES YES YES YES YES
YES YES YES YES YES
YES YES YES YES YES YES
YES YES YES YES YES YES
YES YES YES YES YES YES
YES YES YES YES YES YES
YES YES YES YES YES YES
YES YES YES YES YES YES
YES YES YES YES YES
YES YES YES YES YES YES
YES YES YES YES
YES YES YES YES YES
YES YES YES YES YES
YES YES YES YES YES YES
YES YES YES YES
YES YES YES
YES YES YES
YES YES YES YES
YES
YES

HOME BREW

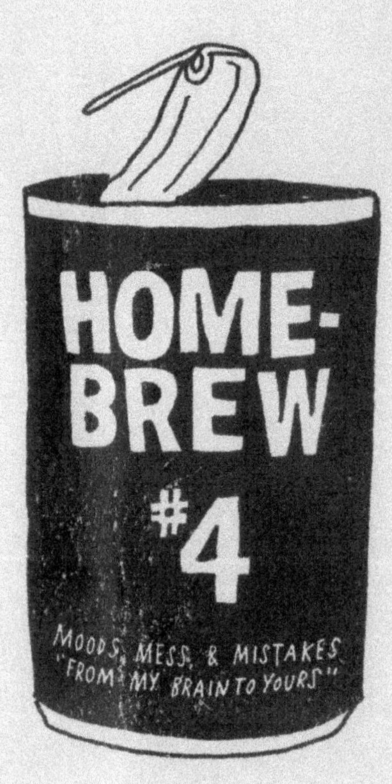

HOME BREW

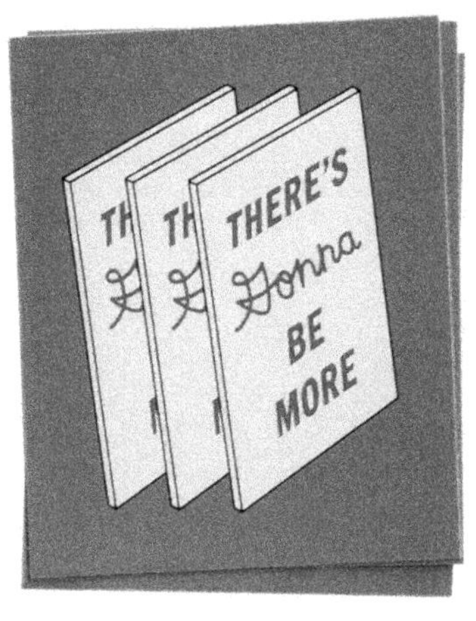

THERE'S
THERE'S
THERE'S
Gonna
BE
MORE

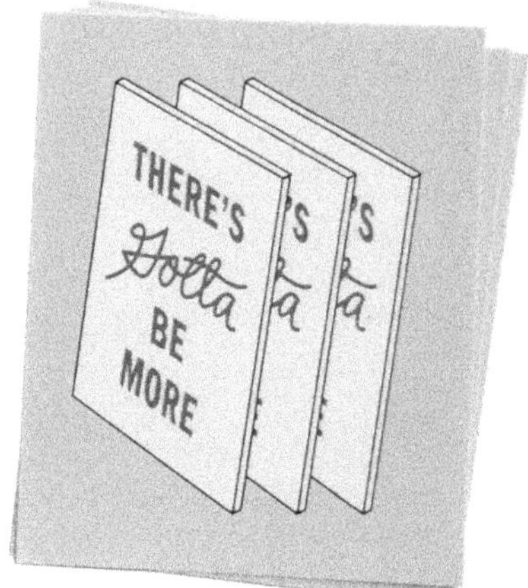

THERE'S
Gotta
BE
MORE
'S
'S

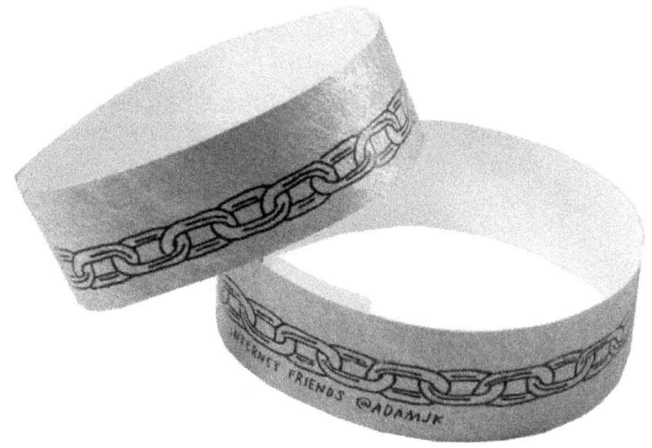

INTERNET FRIENDS @ADAMJK

HOME BREW

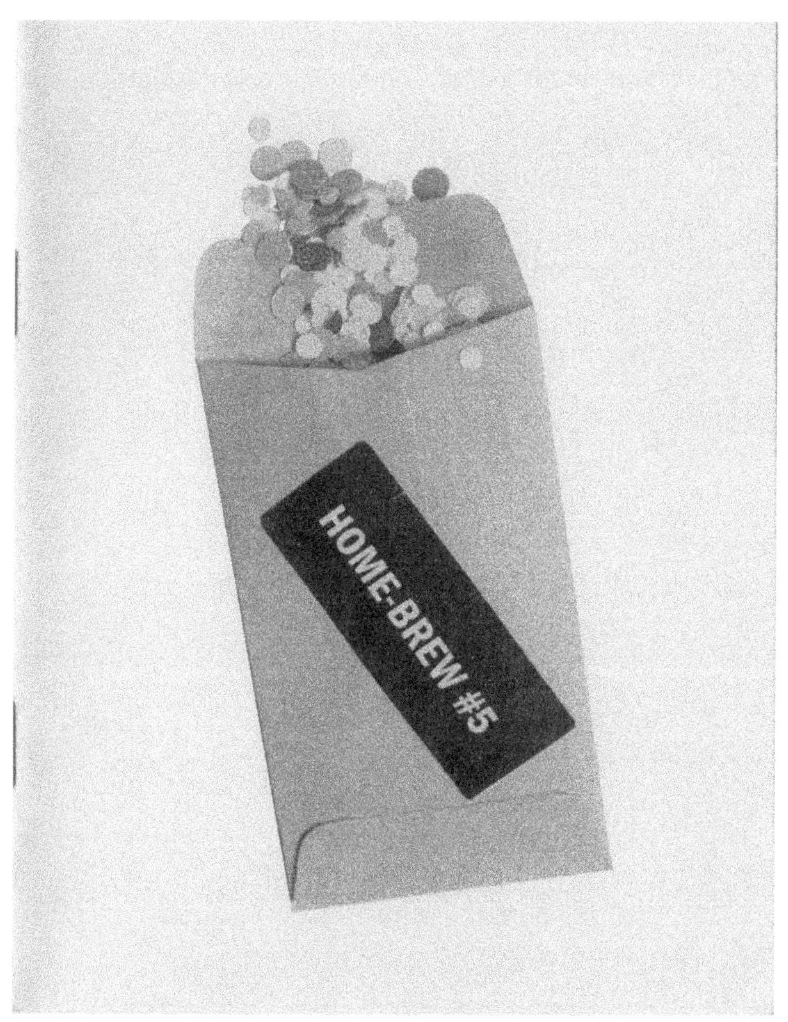

HOME-BREW #5

HOME BREW

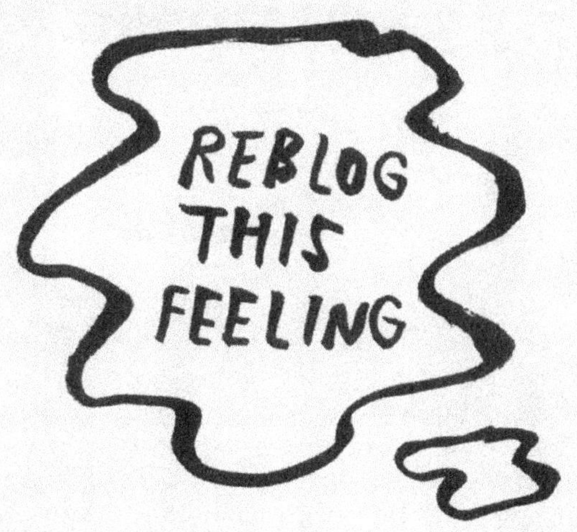

REBLOG
THIS
FEELING

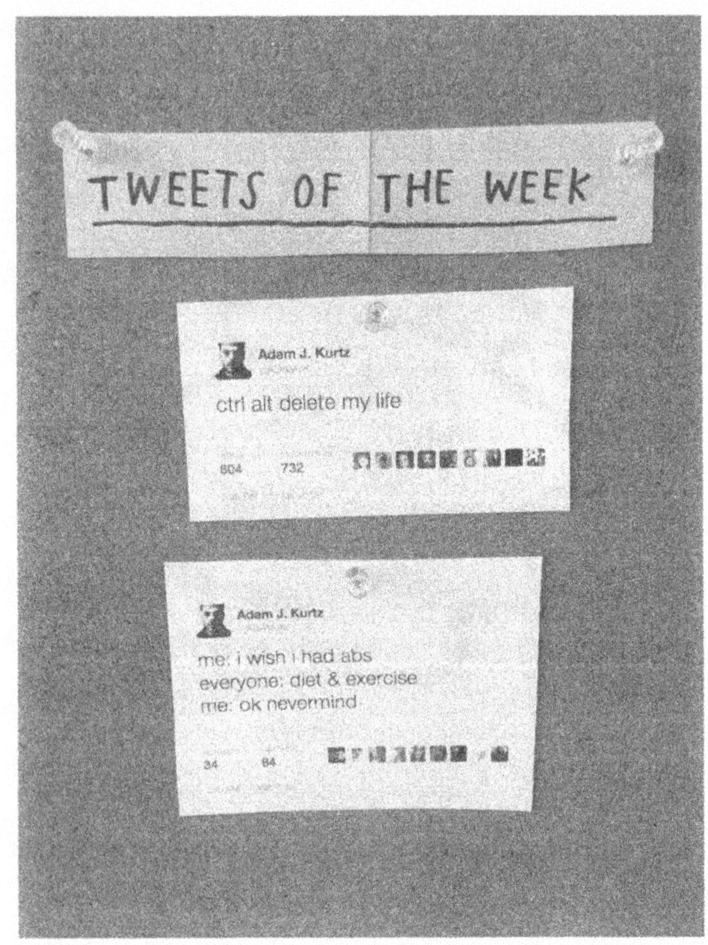

TWEETS OF THE WEEK
Adam J. Kurtz
ctrl alt delete my life
604   732
Adam J. Kurtz
me: i wish i had abs
everyone: diet & exercise
me: ok nevermind
34   84

HOME BREW

R.I.P.
CONTENT
(THE FEELING)

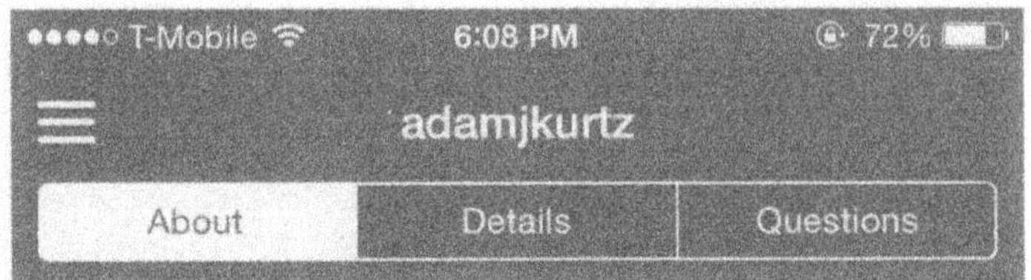

My self-summary

if you want to make me laugh, describe me as "successful," "cool," or "handsome." if you want to date me for 4 days, describe me as all 3.

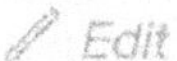

What I'm doing with my life

HOME BREW

I FORGOT MY
PHONE & HONESTL
DON'T KNOW HOW
TO JUST SIT HERE
LIKE WHAT DO I
DO W/ MY HANDS?

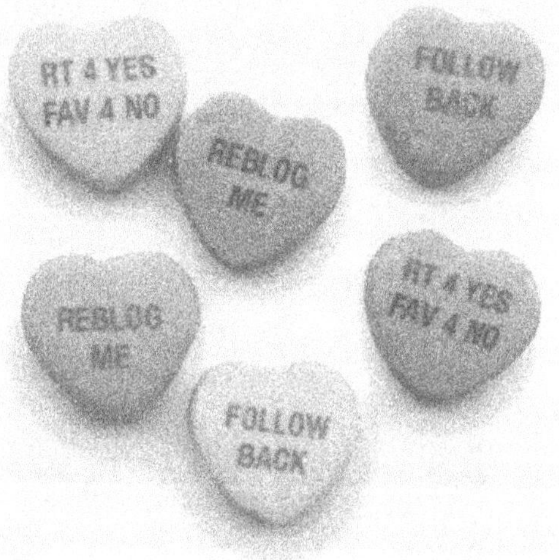

RT 4 YES
FAV 4 NO
REBLOG
ME
FOLLOW
BACK
REBLOG
ME
FOLLOW
BACK
RT 4 YES
FAV 4 NO

HOME BREW

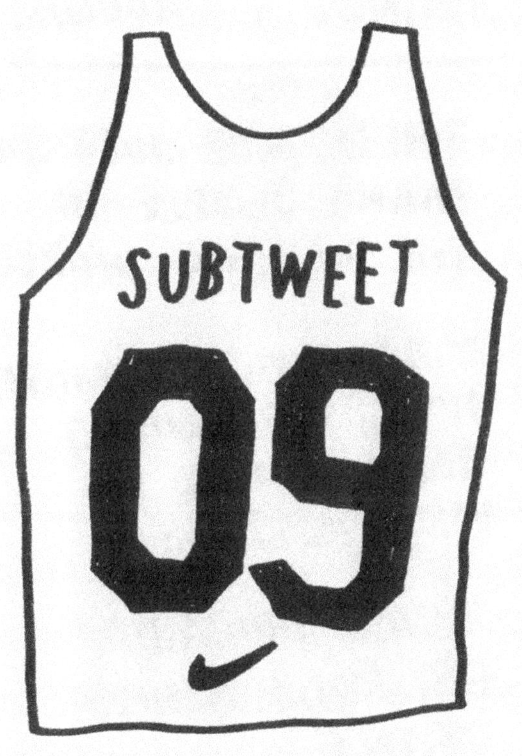

SUBTWEET
09

THINGS I THOUGHT

- THERE ARE JUST SO MANY PEOPLE IN THE FUCKING WORLD

- TODAY HAS SO MANY HOURS LEFT WHAT AM I GONNA DO WITH MYSELF

- I CAN PROBABLY EAT THIS WHOLE THING

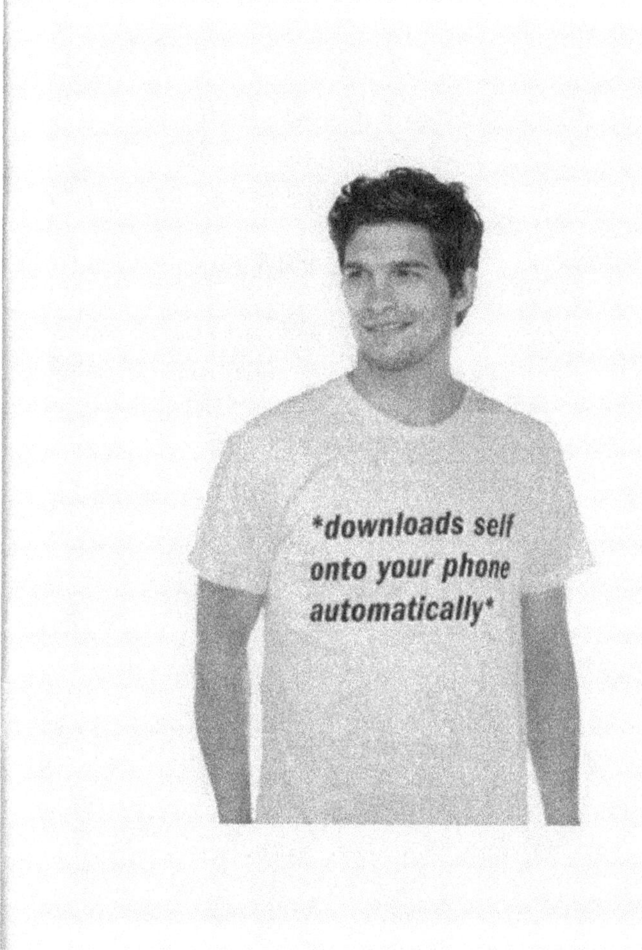

*downloads self
onto your phone
automatically*

IMPORTANT
CARDBOARD

LIMITED
EDITION

SUITABLE
FOR FRAMING
OR HANG AS-IS

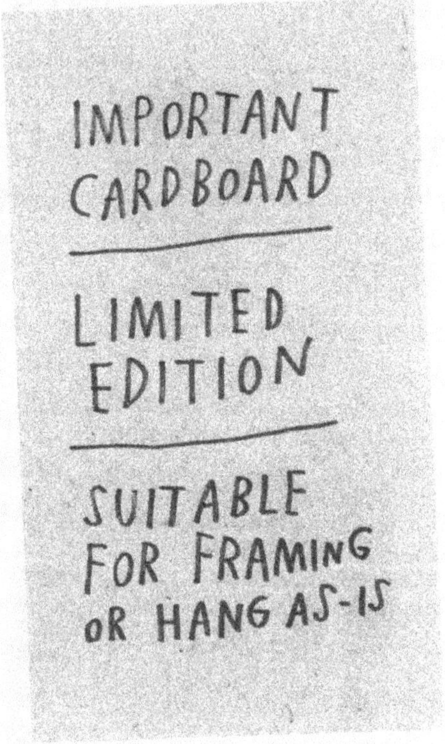

HOME BREW

ALL I WANT RIGHT
NOW IS A DONUT
AMBIEN CIGARETTE
CHEESEBURGER SOFT
SERVE BANANA PANCAKE
SOUR PATCH DARK
CHOCOLATE TANGIBLE
SKILLS HASH BROWN

-@ADAMJK 12:52AM

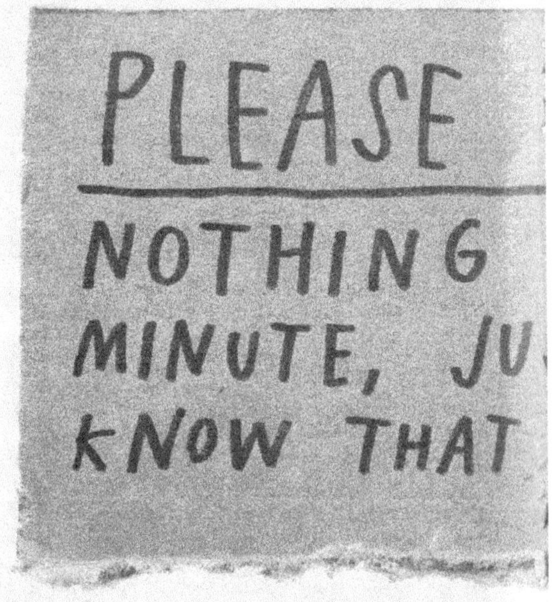

HOME BREW

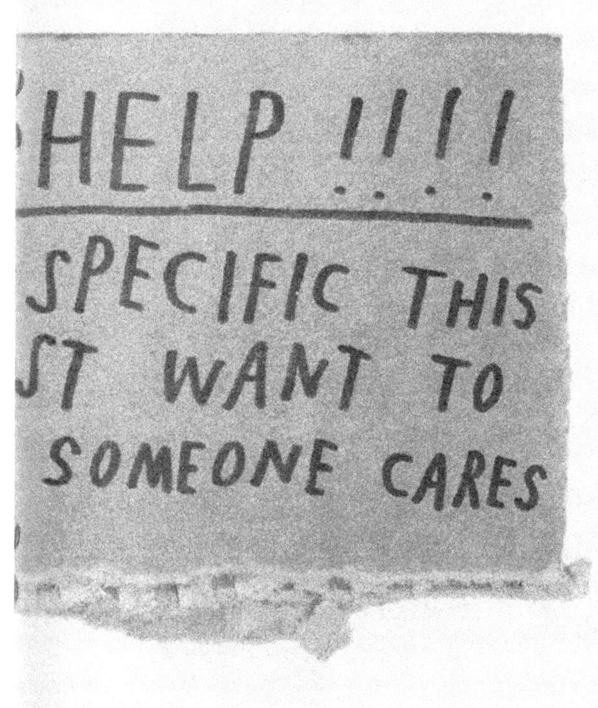
HELP !!!!
SPECIFIC THIS
ST WANT TO
SOMEONE CARES

I'M TRYING TO REMEMBER
THE LAST TIME I WAS
REALLY DISAPPOINTED & I
ACTUALLY CAN'T.

MAYBE I'VE BECOME GOOD
AT MANAGING MY EXPE-
CTATION? MAYBE I HAVE
PRACTICE IN BEING
REALISTIC?

THE TRUTH IS THAT I MAY
ACTUALLY JUST BE LUCKY.
I HAVE WHAT I NEED &
PLENTY I WANT. WHAT'S
TO BE DISAPPOINTED ABOUT?

HOME BREW

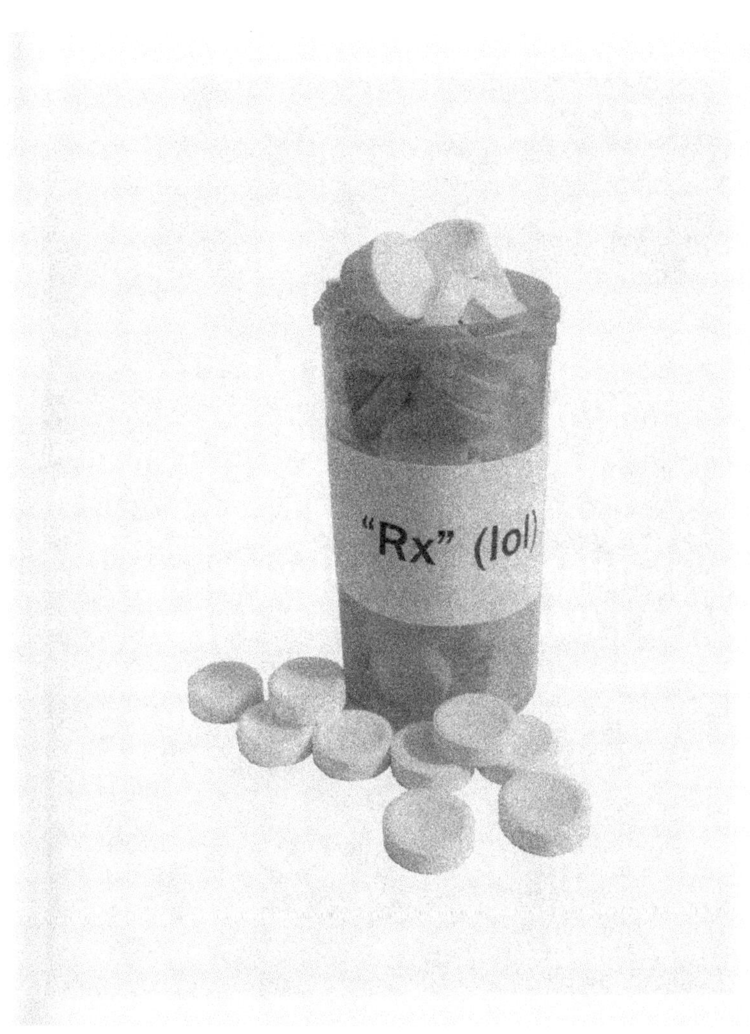

"Rx" (lol)

I LIKE TO TAKE TIME EACH
NIGHT TO FIRST process
THE INDIVIDUAL MOMENTS
EXPERIENCED THAT DAY &
THEN regret THE CHOICES
I MADE IN MOST OF THEM

-@ADAMJK, 12:17AM

HOME BREW

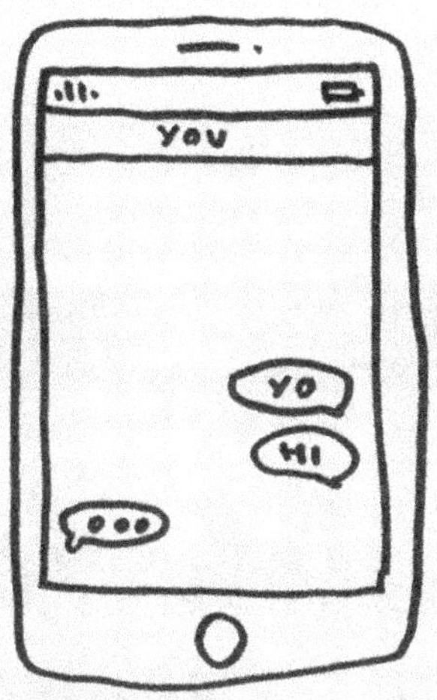

IT'S NICE TO
KNOW THAT
YOU'RE THINKING
OF ME

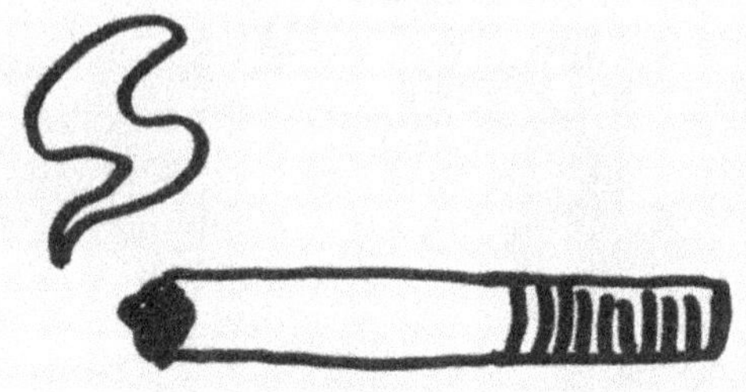

HOME BREW

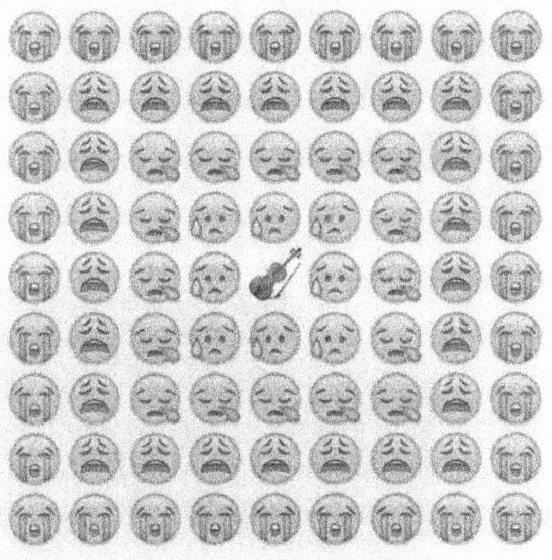

things that don't exist:

a perfectly worded text message sent to everybody I've ever kissed that's both sentimental and appropriate, responded to with helpful insight into who I might be, that acts as a catalyst for positive personal change

HOME BREW

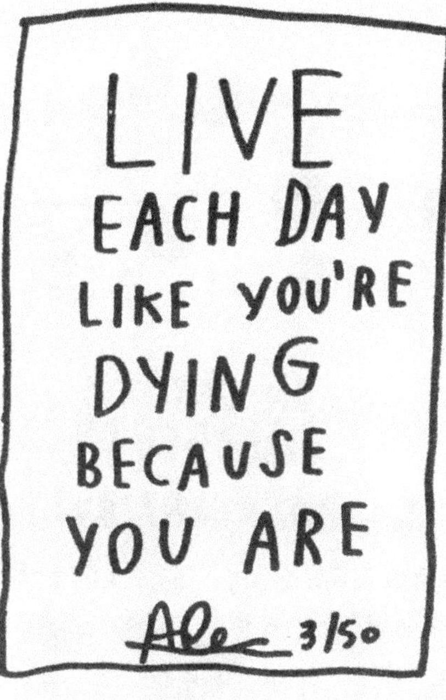

INSPIRATIONAL
LETTERPRESS
PRINT — $200

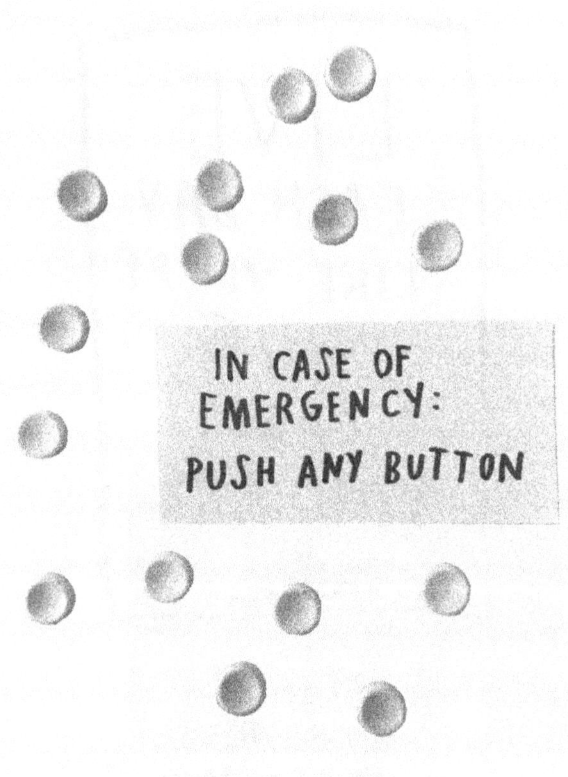

HOME BREW

COOL THINGS
ABOUT ME

- DON'T BITE NAILS
- TALL
- OWN A STAPLER
- TATTOOS
- COMPUTER SKILLS
- HEALTH INSURANCE
- BIG IN BRAZIL
- BAKE BANANA BREAD
- GOOD KISSER

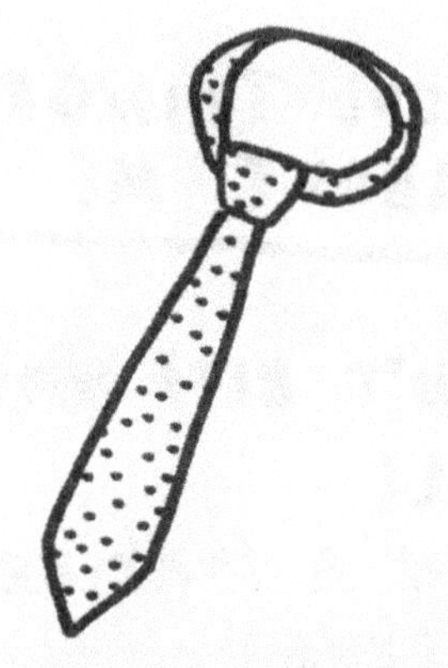

I HOPE I NEVER
ACCOMPLISH
ANYTHING SO I
NEVER HAVE TO
DRESS NICELY

HOME BREW

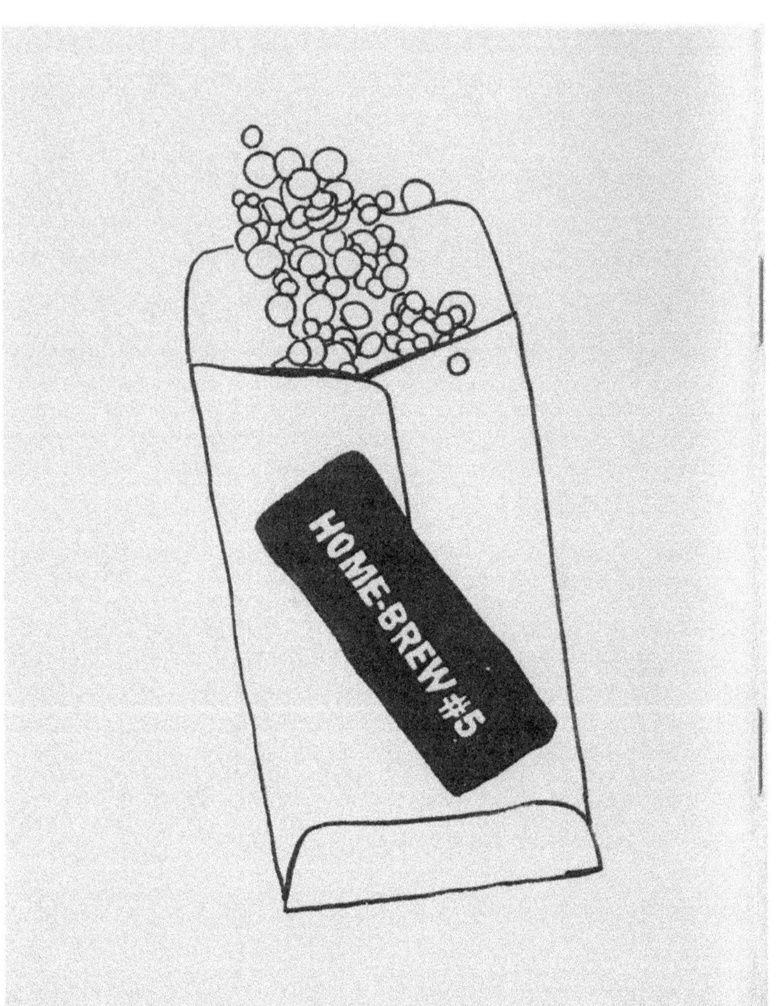

HOME BREW

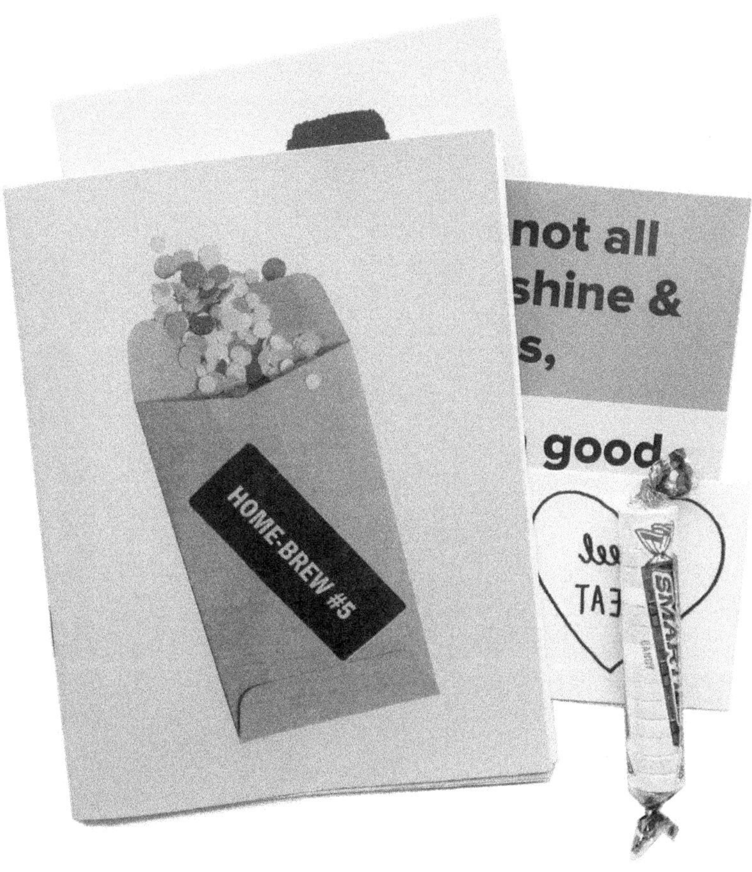
HOME-BREW #5
not all
shine &
s,
good
TAE
SMARTIES

HOME BREW

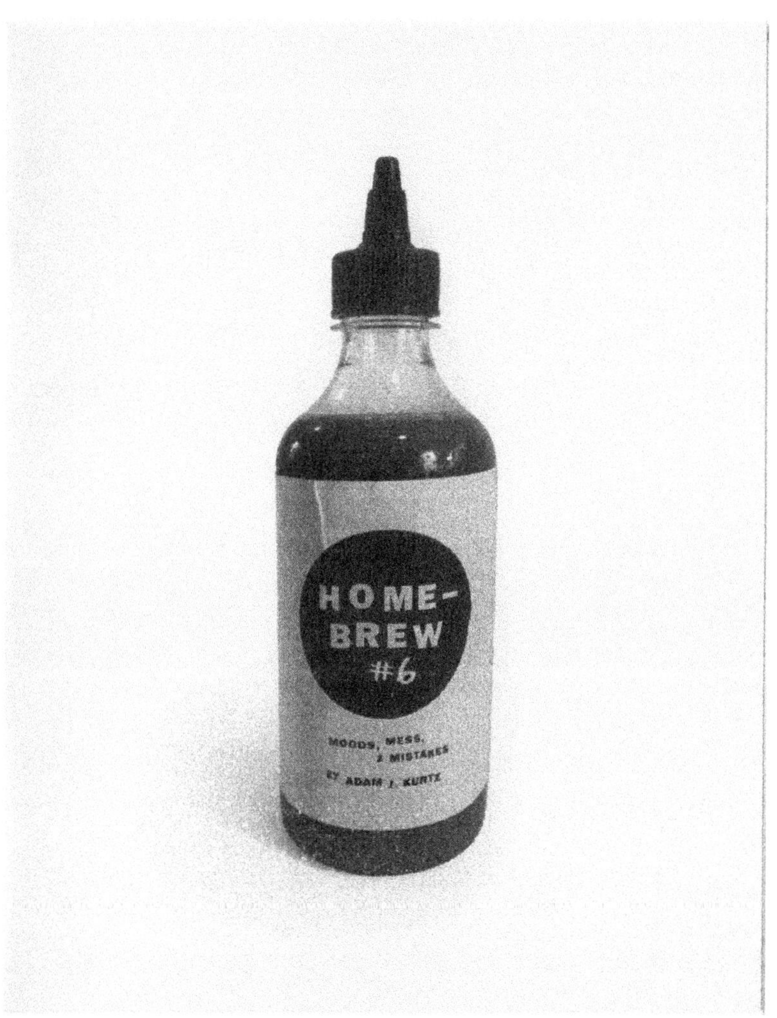
HOME-
BREW
#6
MOODS, MESS,
& MISTAKES
BY ADAM J. KURTZ

HOME BREW

I WOULD LOVE
TO MAKE ART
INSPIRED BY
BEAUTY INSTEAD
OF ANGST BUT I
DON'T UNDERSTAND
BEAUTY YET

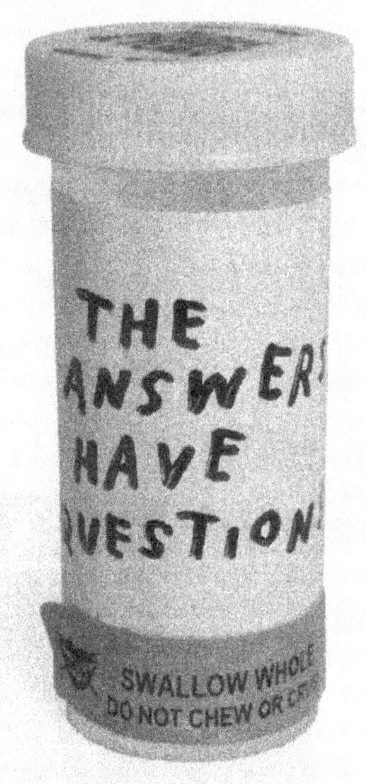

HOME BREW

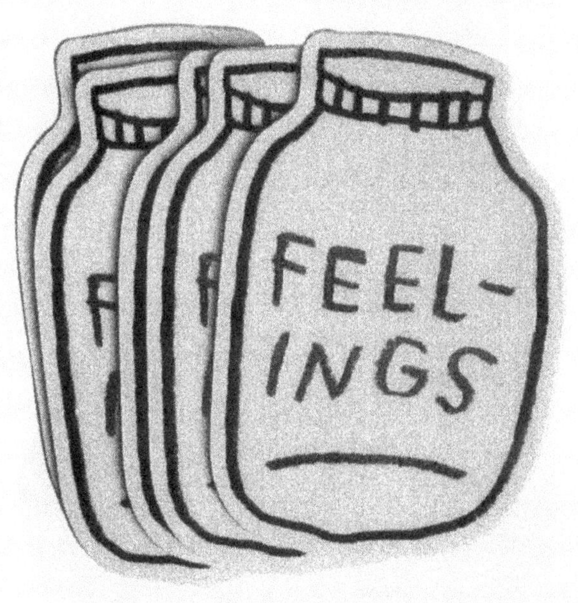

FEEL-
INGS

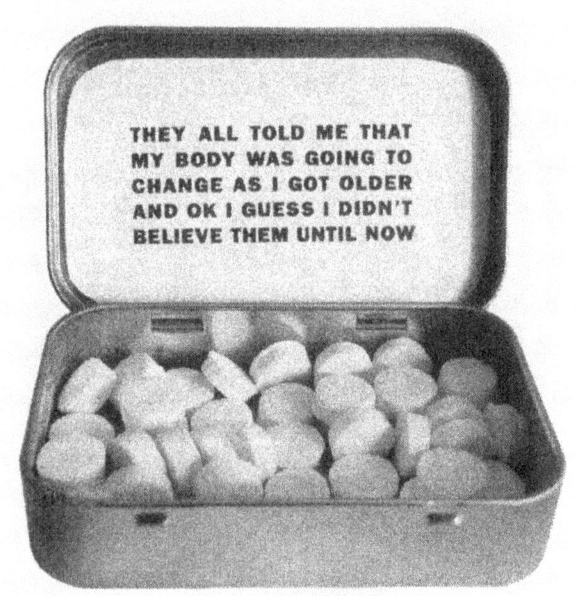
THEY ALL TOLD ME THAT
MY BODY WAS GOING TO
CHANGE AS I GOT OLDER
AND OK I GUESS I DIDN'T
BELIEVE THEM UNTIL NOW

HOME BREW

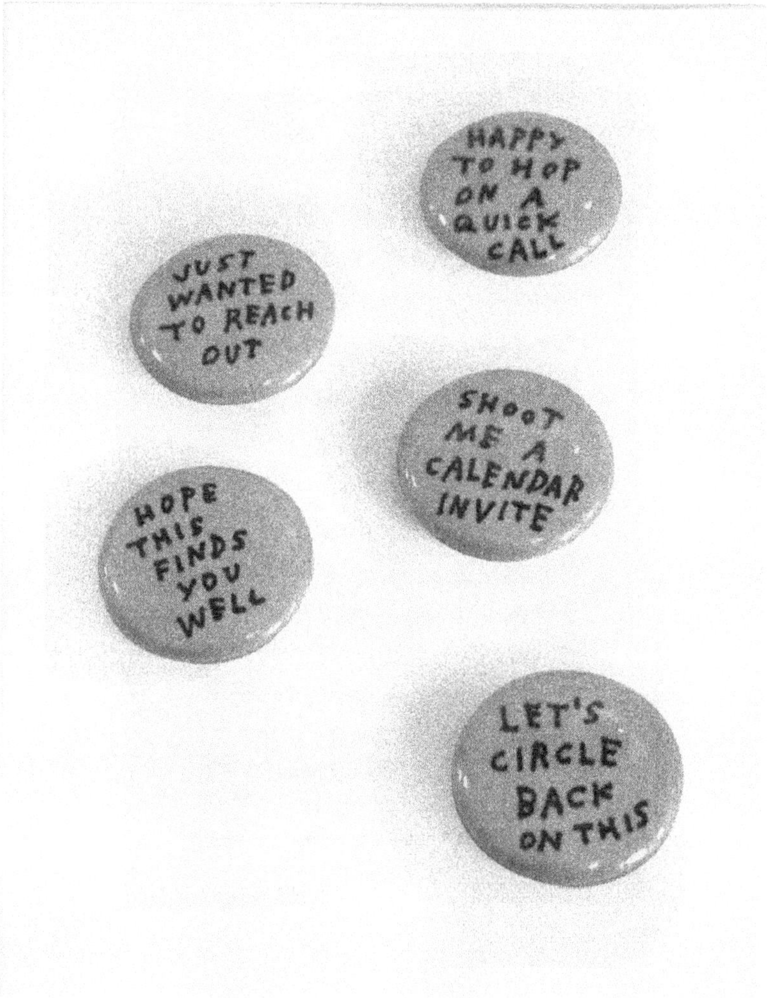

HAPPY TO HOP ON A QUICK CALL
JUST WANTED TO REACH OUT
SHOOT ME A CALENDAR INVITE
HOPE THIS FINDS YOU WELL
LET'S CIRCLE BACK ON THIS

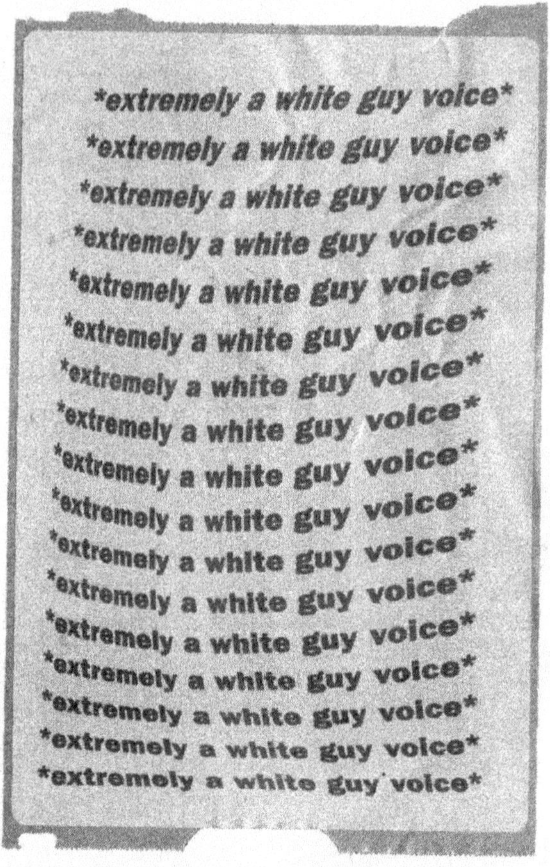

HOME BREW

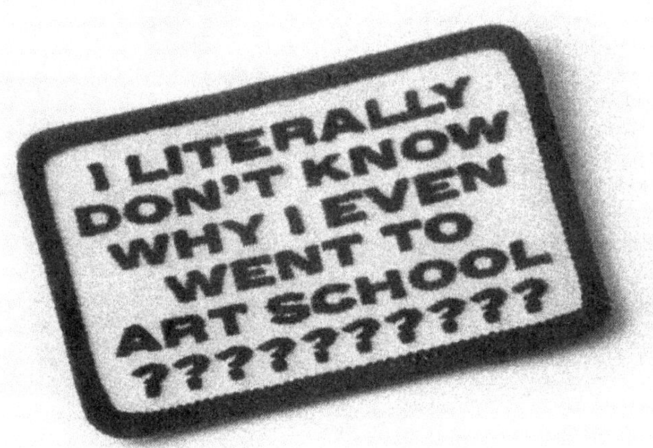

I LITERALLY
DON'T KNOW
WHY I EVEN
WENT TO
ART SCHOOL
???????????

HOME BREW

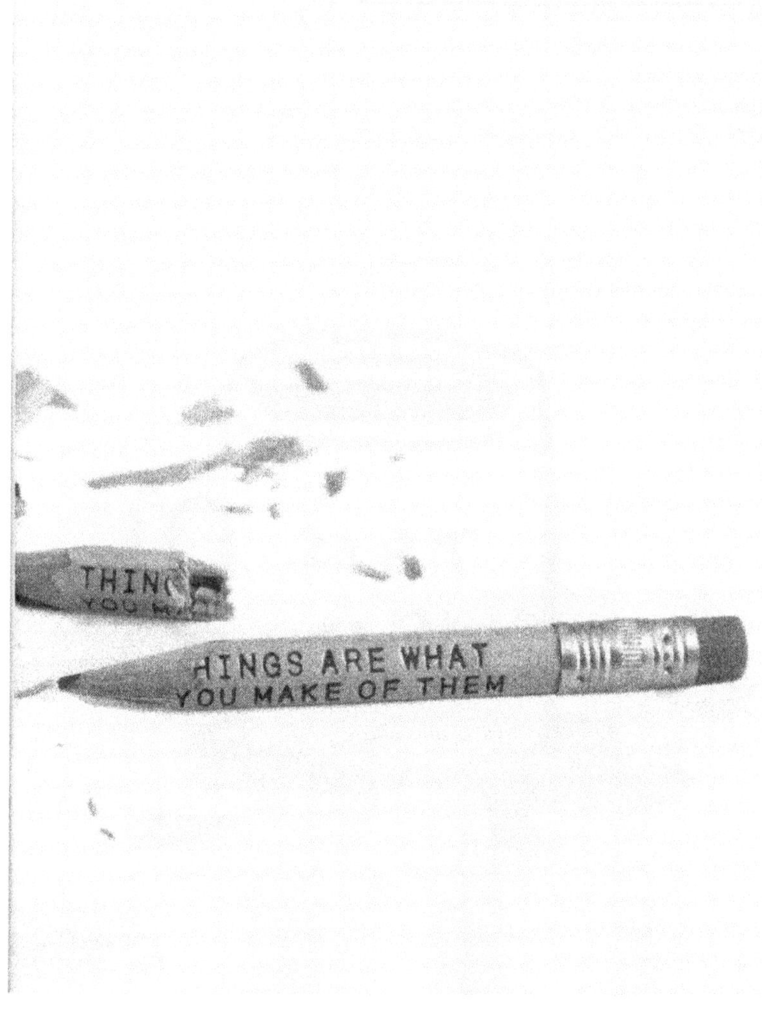
THING
YOU
HINGS ARE WHAT
YOU MAKE OF THEM

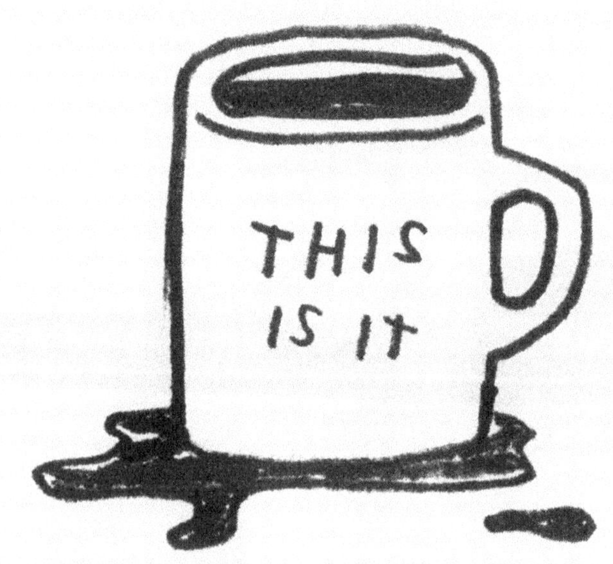

HOME BREW

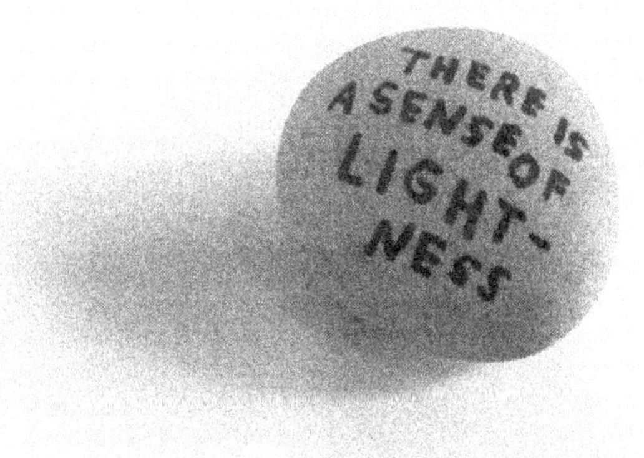

THERE IS
A SENSE OF
LIGHT-
NESS

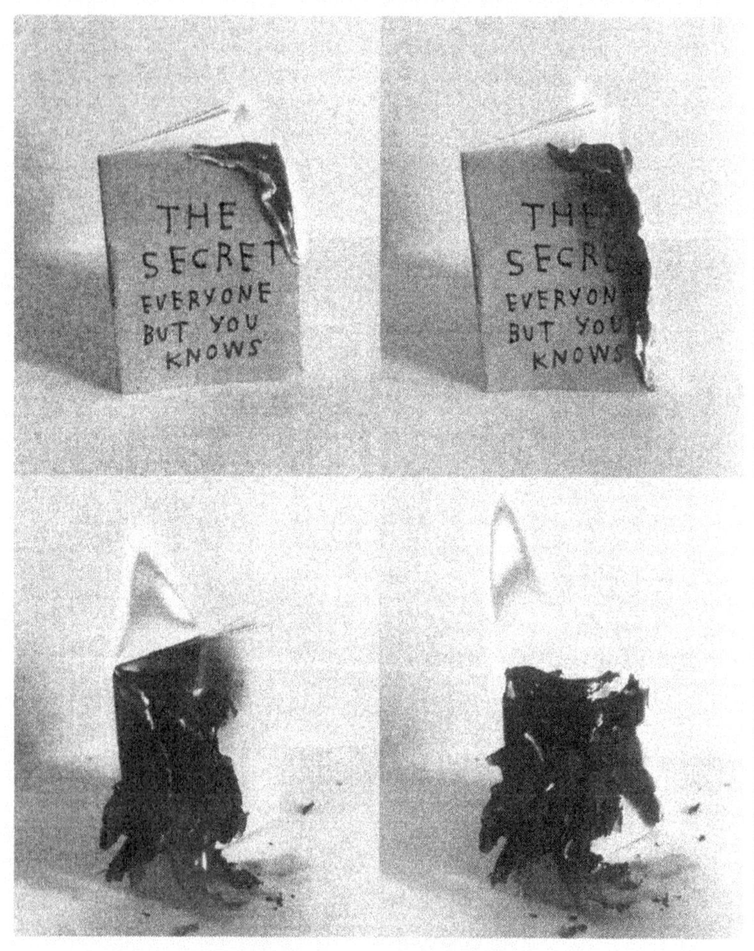
THE
SECRET
EVERYONE
BUT YOU
KNOWS
THE
SECR
EVERYON
BUT YOU
KNOWS

HOME BREW

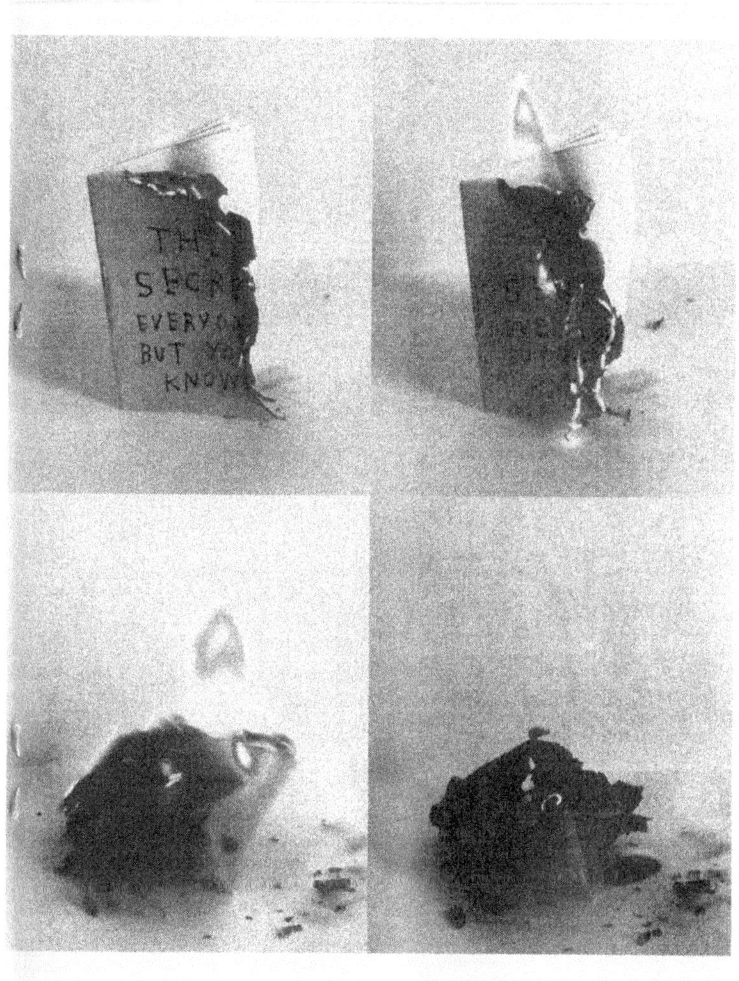
THE
SECRET
EVERYO
BUT YO
KNOW

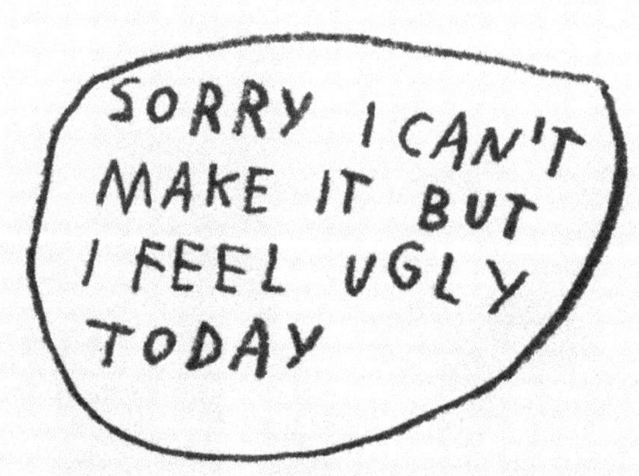

HOME BREW

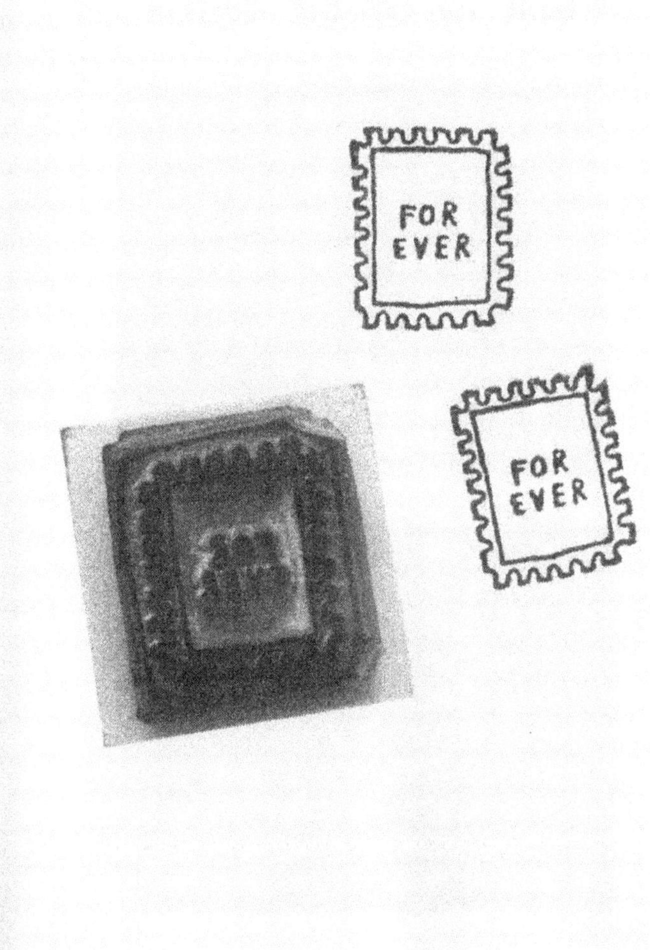

FOR
EVER
FOR
EVER

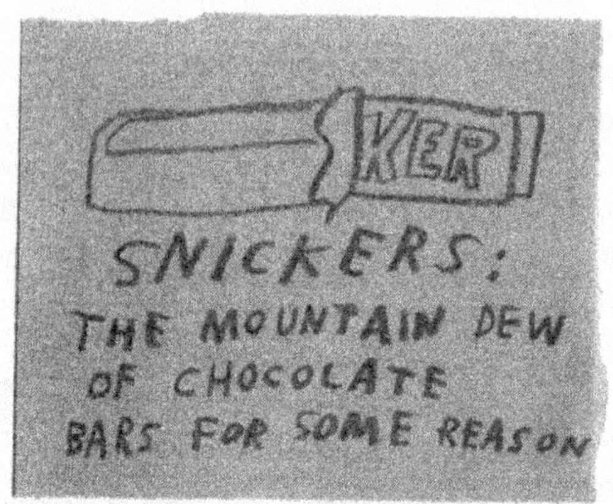
SNICKERS:
THE MOUNTAIN DEW
OF CHOCOLATE
BARS FOR SOME REASON

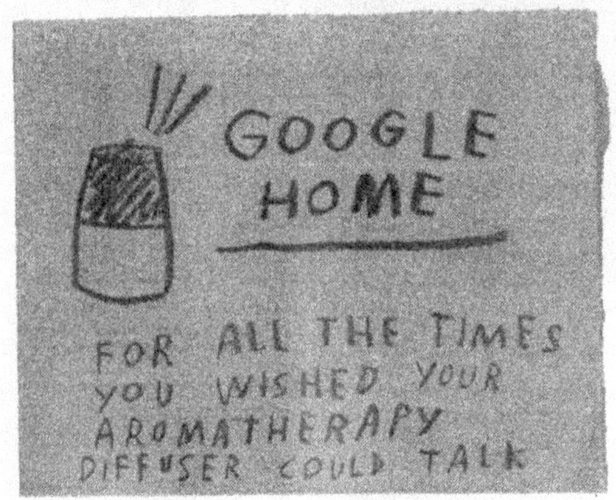
GOOGLE
HOME

FOR ALL THE TIMES
YOU WISHED YOUR
AROMATHERAPY
DIFFUSER COULD TALK

HOME BREW

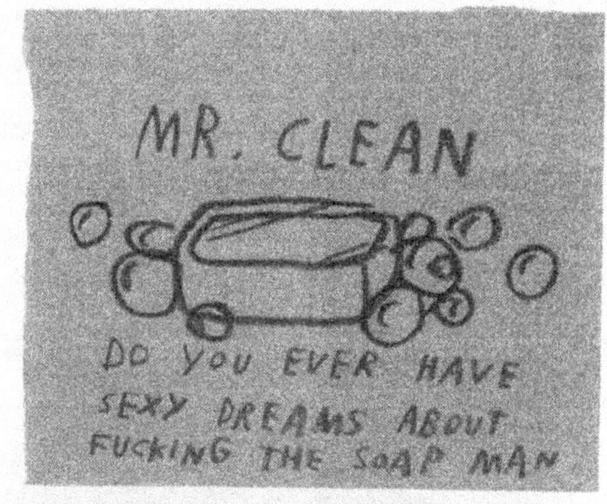
MR. CLEAN
DO YOU EVER HAVE
SEXY DREAMS ABOUT
FUCKING THE SOAP MAN

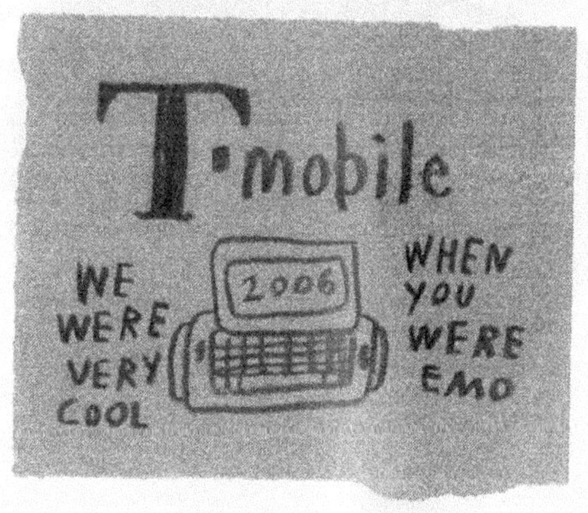
T·mobile
WE
WERE
VERY
COOL
2006
WHEN
YOU
WERE
EMO

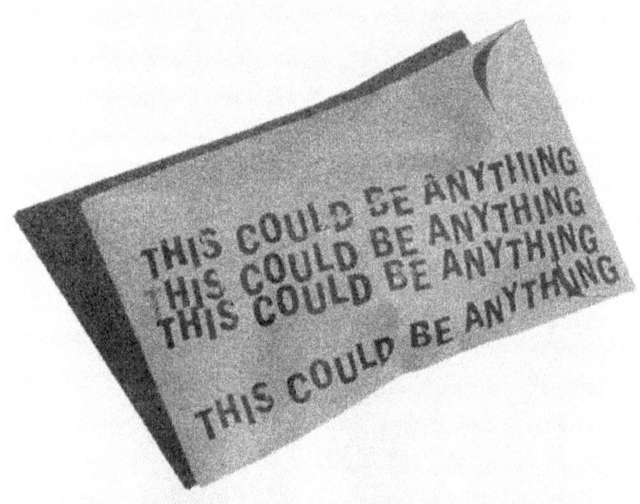

THIS COULD BE ANYTHING
THIS COULD BE ANYTHING
THIS COULD BE ANYTHING
THIS COULD BE ANYTHING

HOME BREW

REALIZED THAT
THE WAY I FEEL
ABOUT "CONSTANT
MUFFLED MARIACHI
BASSLINE" IS HOW
MY NEIGHBOR
MUST FEEL ABOUT
ALANIS MORISSETTE'S
ENTIRE
DISCOGRAPHY

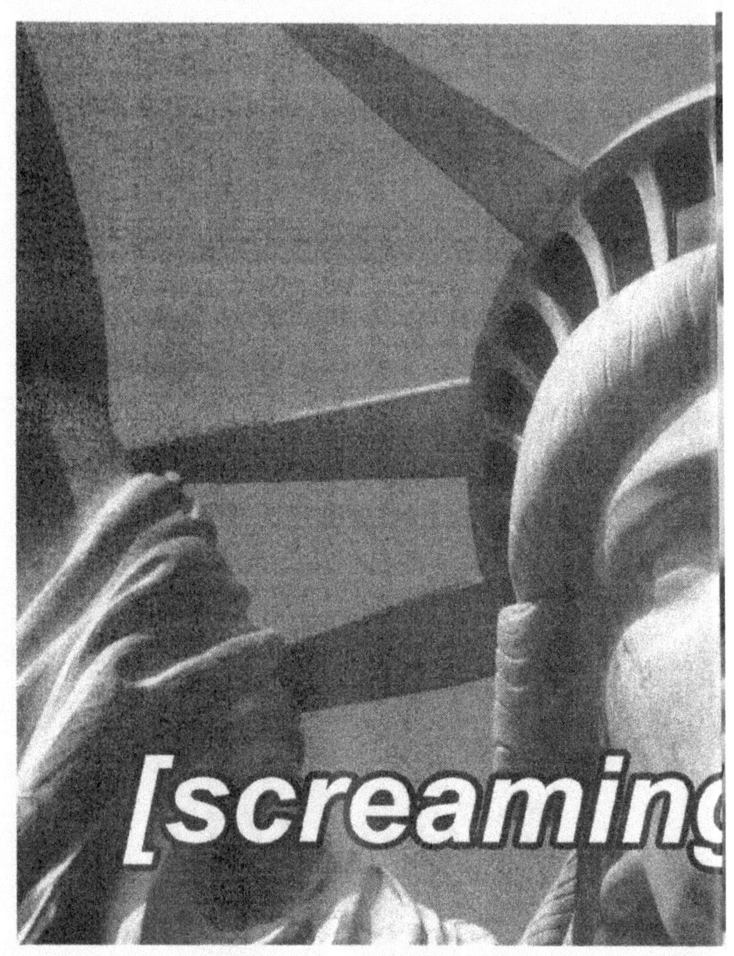

HOME BREW

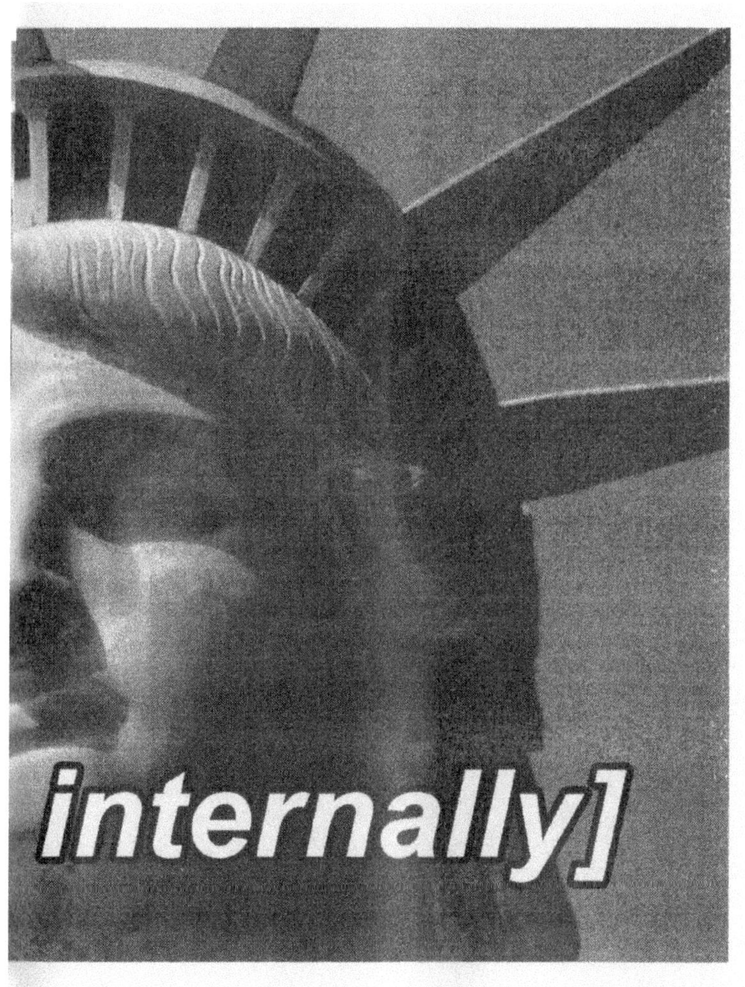
internally]

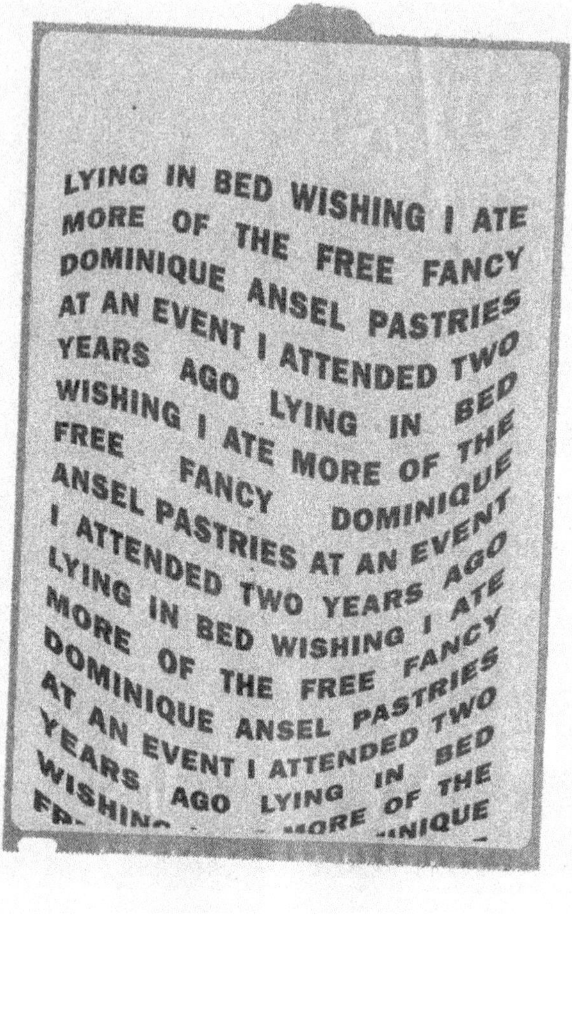

LYING IN BED WISHING I ATE
MORE OF THE FREE FANCY
DOMINIQUE ANSEL PASTRIES
AT AN EVENT I ATTENDED TWO
YEARS AGO LYING IN BED
WISHING I ATE MORE OF THE
FREE FANCY DOMINIQUE
ANSEL PASTRIES AT AN EVENT
I ATTENDED TWO YEARS AGO
LYING IN BED WISHING I ATE
MORE OF THE FREE FANCY
DOMINIQUE ANSEL PASTRIES
AT AN EVENT I ATTENDED TWO
YEARS AGO LYING IN BED
WISHING MORE OF THE
FREE DOMINIQUE

HOME BREW

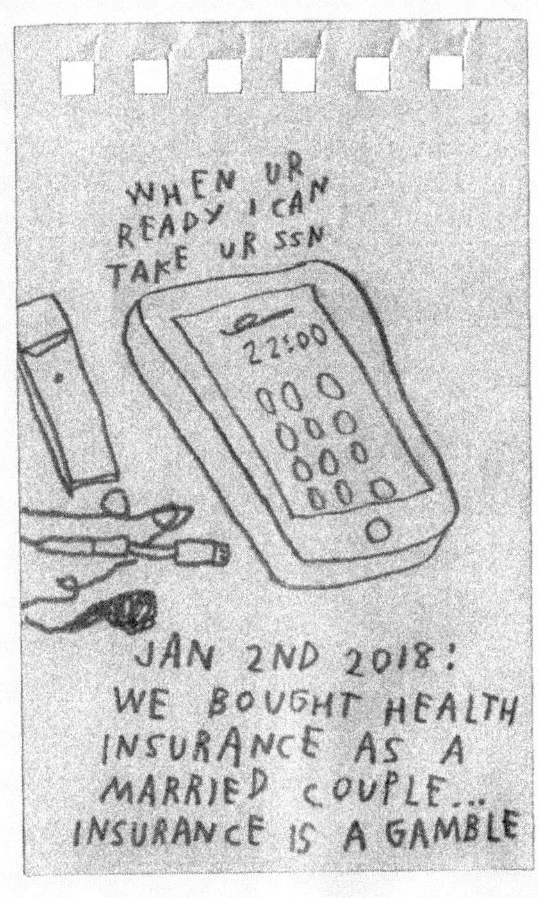

WHEN UR READY I CAN TAKE UR SSN
22:00
JAN 2ND 2018:
WE BOUGHT HEALTH INSURANCE AS A MARRIED COUPLE... INSURANCE IS A GAMBLE

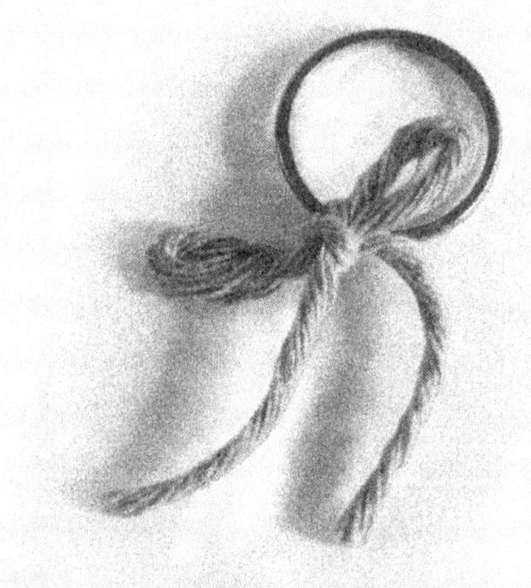

HOME BREW

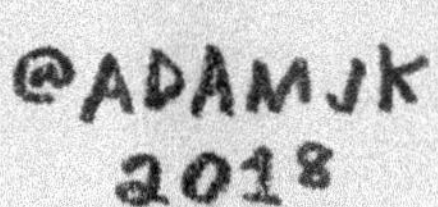

HOME BREW

The Museum of Modern Art

11 West 53 Street, New York, NY 10019

Purch

No.

PENDING APPROVAL

VENDOR: ADAM J KURTZ
         36 LINDEN ST #98
         BROOKLYN   NY

         11221

ATTN: ADAM J KURTZ

SHIP TO: MOMA DES
          11 WEST
          NEW YORK
          10019

NOTE:

Buyer	Vendor MoMA Ac#	F.O.B.	Term
NORMAN LAURILA		USA	

MoMA Item#	Quantity	Description/Style Number
114123	15	ZINE HOME BREW 4 ADAM KURTZ HOMEBREW ZINE 4
114124	15	ZINE HOME BREW 5 ADAM KURTZ HOMEBREW ZINE 5
114125	50	NOTEBOOK LADDER ADAM KURTZ NB LADDER SHIP DATE- 6/13/15 CANC

HOME BREW

Word up

Feast your eyes on some of the one-of-a-kind mags you'll find at the Brooklyn Zine Fest. By **Jillian Anthony**

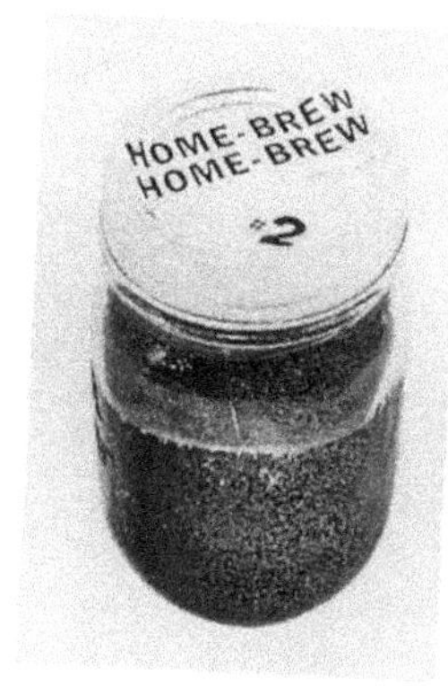

Home-Brew

Adam J. Kurtz brings several of his quirky print products to this year's fest. His flagship zine, *Home-Brew*, comes packaged with a "sad birthday loot bag" filled with stickers, a postcard print, mini-pencils and other surprises related to the issue.

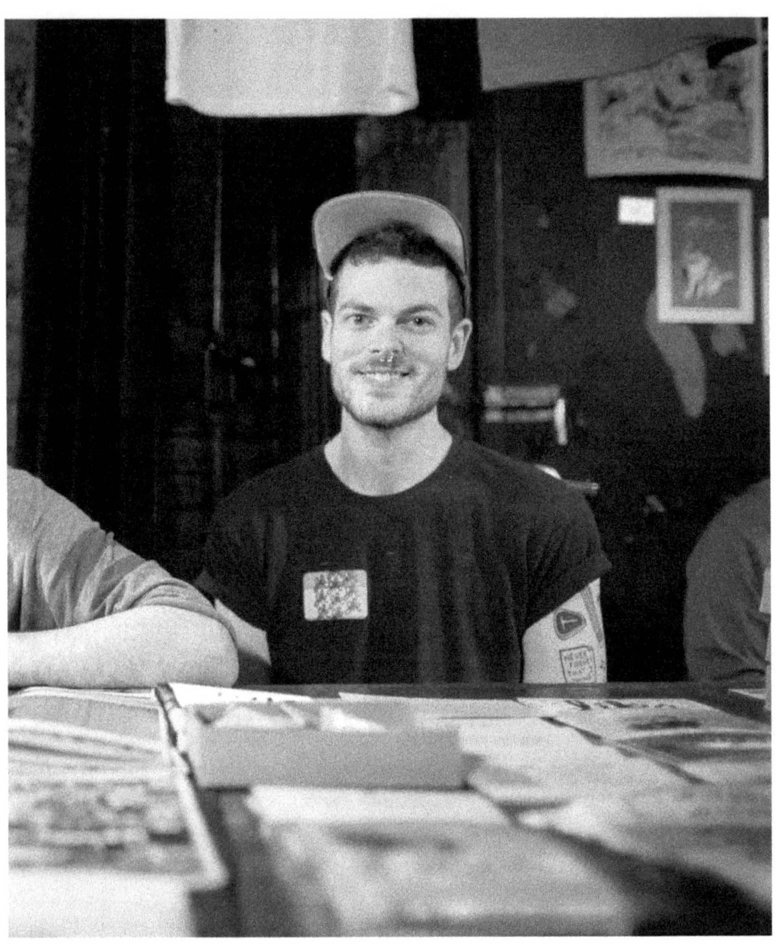

Brooklyn Zine Fest 2013
Photo by Steve McFarland (stevetm.com)

HOME BREW

ACKNOWLEDGEMENTS

Thank you to everyone who's purchased a copy of this book, or any of the zines over the years, or anything else I've made literally ever. Nobody starts making zines and multiples expecting to financially support themselves, much less build a career doing it. I'll be forever grateful that my weird little offering has been received positively by others. Thank you for making good things happen for me and for helping me feel less alone in my brain and in the world.

A special thank you to the people who make space for art from young and emerging artists of all kinds:

Stockists like Atomic Books, Trohv, Quimby's, Wonder Fair, Desert Island, and BuyOlympia (whose early support encouraged me to keep growing, and events including Brooklyn Zine Fest and Pete's Mini Zine Fest, which gave me the chance to see what was possible (almost anything) and connect with others.

It also seems worth acknowledging that I have been (and continue to be) rejected by "gatekeepers" of all kinds. This has never stopped me from making things anyway. This book, like the zines reprinted within, is self-published. It's all just paper!

ADAM J. KURTZ

Adam J. Kurtz is an artist and author whose illustrative work is rooted in honesty, humor and a little darkness.

His books, including *1 Page at a Time* and *Things Are What You Make of Them,* have been translated into over a dozen languages worldwide. He is still trying.

For more from Adam, visit adamjk.com or @adamjk.